Cross Training

Ultimate Fitness

Fitness, Health & Nutrition was created by Rebus, Inc. and published by Time-Life Books.

REBUS, INC.

Publisher: RODNEY FRIEDMAN
Editorial Director: CHARLES L. MEE JR.

Editor: THOMAS DICKEY
Senior Editor: MARK CROWLEY
Text Editor: LINDA EPSTEIN
Associate Editors: WILLIAM DUNNETT, CARL LOWE
Chief of Research: CARNEY W. MIMMS III
Copy Editor: ROBERT HERNANDEZ
Contributing Editors: JACQUELINE DAMIAN, JANE SCHECHTER

Art Director: JUDITH HENRY
Associate Art Director: FRANCINE KASS
Designer: SARA BOWMAN
Still Life and Food Photographer: STEVEN MAYS
Exercise Photographer: ANDREW ECCLES
Photo Stylist: LEAH LOCOCO
Contributing Photographer: DAVID MADISON

Test Kitchen Director: GRACE YOUNG
Recipe Editor: BONNIE J. SLOTNICK

TIME-LIFE BOOKS

Editor-in-Chief (Europe): Sue Joiner
European Executive Editor: Gillian Moore
Design Director: Ed Skyner
Assistant Design Director: Mary Staples
Chief of Research: Vanessa Kramer
Chief Sub-Editor: Ilse Gray

EUROPEAN EDITION

Designer: Paul Reeves
Sub-Editors: Lindsay McTeague, Wendy Toole
Chief of Editorial Production: Maureen Kelly
Production Assistant: Samantha Hill
Editorial Department: Theresa John, Debra Lelliott

FITNESS, HEALTH & NUTRITION

Cross Training
Ultimate Fitness

Time-Life Books, Amsterdam

CONSULTANTS FOR THIS BOOK

Paul Asmuth, a world champion marathon swimmer, has won every major swimming marathon at least once and holds the record for five events. He also set a men's world record for swimming the English Channel.

Richard A. Berger, Ph.D., is professor of exercise physiology at the College of Health, Physical Education, Recreation and Dance at Temple University in Philadelphia.

John Howard has been a competitive cyclist and triathlete for the past 20 years. A seven-time United States Cycling Federation champion and a Pan-American Games gold medalist, Howard set a world speed record for cycling at 245 km/h.

Amy Lyn Kallman, M.A., is the director of public fitness programmes at Sports Training Institute in New York City. She is also a private fitness consultant.

Dave Scott is a triathlete whom many consider to be the premier endurance athlete in the world today. He is a six-time winner and undisputed master of the gruelling Ironman triathlon, which is held annually in Hawaii, and he has won or been placed in numerous other national and international triathlons.

William Wagner is an exercise specialist at Sports Training Institute, New York City.

John White, Ph.D., is Reader in Human Performance and Health Studies at the University of Ulster at Jordanstown, Northern Ireland, with responsibilities for undergraduate teaching and postgraduate research in exercise and health physiology.

Nutritional consultants:

Ann Grandjean, Ed. D., is chief nutrition consultant to the U.S. Olympic Committee and an instructor in the Sports Medicine Program, University of Nebraska Medical Center.

Myron Winick, M.D., is Professor of Nutrition at Columbia University College of Physicians and Surgeons, New York.

ISBN 0 7054 0728 4

TIME-LIFE is a trademark of Time Warner Inc. U.S.A.

This book is not intended as a substitute for the advice of a doctor or an athletic coach. Readers who have or suspect they may have specific medical problems should consult a doctor before beginning any programme of strenuous physical exercise.

CONTENTS

CHAPTER ONE

Total Conditioning

The benefits — and pleasures — of expanding your training programme

Many people, when they take up exercise, find themselves choosing and sticking with a single activity or workout. However, a growing number of athletes and fitness enthusiasts are expanding their regimens through cross training — building and maintaining fitness by training in more than one activity. The benefits of cross training range from injury prevention to relief from boredom, and this chapter presents the merits, the challenges and the debates about this relatively new method of rounding out an exercise programme. It will also show you how to practise cross training in a manageable schedule. Because many cross trainers begin primarily as runners, the exercise chapters in this book focus largely on cycling and swimming, the two most popular alternatives for building aerobic fitness. And if you want to compete, you can use this overview of cross training as your guide to combine all three activities into a training programme for a triathlon — the ultimate test of conditioning for strength, versatility and endurance.

Cross Training: a Total-Body Regimen

Training in a variety of sports conditions many more muscles than any one sport can. The illustrations show the primary and secondary muscle groups (primary muscles are those that are used directly to perform an activity; secondary muscles assist the primary muscle group) exercised in swimming, cycling and running. In a cross-training programme, each activity complements the others in building overall strength and muscular endurance. Swimming primarily conditions the upper body muscles, which are directly responsible for propulsion. Cycling relies mainly on front of thigh and back muscles, while running emphasizes opposing muscles along the back of the leg.

Primary muscle groups ●
Secondary muscle groups ●

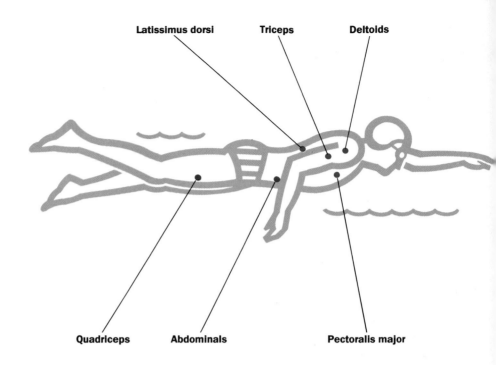

Latissimus dorsi   Triceps   Deltoids

Quadriceps   Abdominals   Pectoralis major

Who uses cross training?

In recent years, many athletes, especially endurance athletes, have claimed that the fitness benefits derived from training in several sports or modes of exercise can result in better overall conditioning as well as improved performance in one or more of the activities. To what extent cross training can increase performance potential is widely debated. Other benefits, as discussed below, are more clear cut, and certainly cross training has become a popular method of staying fit. Runners are particularly drawn to some form of cross training: in a survey of recreational runners, more than 90 per cent reported that they habitually engaged in another sport or endurance activity, with cycling and swimming the leading preferences. And since the late 1970s, cross training — or expanded training, as it is also sometimes called — has been popularized as the exercise regimen used by triathletes, who typically train and compete in swimming, cycling and running, and are considered by many experts to be the best-conditioned athletes in the world.

Unless you want to be a triathlete, is cross training really a worthwhile pursuit?

Anyone who is intent on maintaining a programme of aerobic exercise can derive benefits from cross training. One compelling reason for

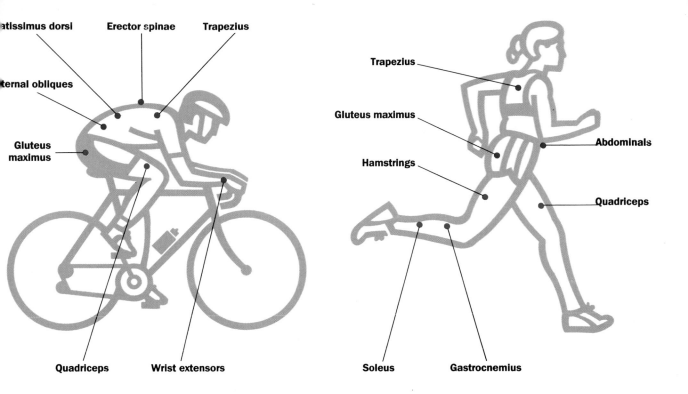

Latissimus dorsi   Erector spinae   Trapezius

Internal obliques

Gluteus
maximus

Quadriceps   Wrist extensors

Trapezius

Gluteus maximus

Hamstrings

Abdominals

Quadriceps

Soleus   Gastrocnemius

runners to cross train is that substituting activities such as cycling and swimming for some of their workout runs will diffuse the physical stress of running, thereby reducing the risk of injury. Not only are swimming and cycling low-impact activities compared to running, but each conditions distinctly different muscle groups as well as exercising some of the same muscles in different ways. In endurance workouts, injuries may result when one muscle group becomes stronger than an opposing group. Doing a greater variety of exercise reduces the chance of creating this kind of imbalance and thus the chance of suffering pulled muscles or knee injuries.

If you do sustain an injury from one activity, you can maintain your cardiovascular conditioning while you recover by training in another activity that exercises different muscles. Swimming is excellent for either runners or cyclists who suffer leg injuries, since the driving force of swimming is powered by the muscles of the upper body. In addition, swimming helps develop your upper and lower body more uniformly than running or cycling alone.

Performing two or three different endurance exercises also affords a mental change of pace that can make working out more enjoyable. If you are starting a new activity, you will usually experience relatively rapid improvement, which is also a great motivator. Finally, whether you cross train to supplement a primary exercise or devote

How Training Affects Muscles

- More and larger capillaries, which deliver a greater volume of blood to working muscles

- Increased stores of energy (glycogen)

- Enlargement of slow-twitch fibres (needed for endurance) and of fast-twitch fibres (for power)

- Mitochondria (the structures within cells that release energy by breaking down phosphate molecules) larger and more numerous

- Less reliance on anaerobic energy systems, with a resulting decrease in lactic acid and muscle fatigue

Muscles undergo profound cellular and metabolic changes with training, as shown in the chart above. The increase in capillaries and changes in mitochondria allow a muscle to use oxygen more effectively, while the improved retention of glycogen (the stored form of carbohydrate) means more energy for work. Muscle fibre contraction is faster and stronger. Also, the fibres do not tire as easily, in part because of the more efficient processing of lactic acid, a by-product of energy metabolism associated with fatigue.

equal amounts of effort to several activities, you will feel in greater overall shape and have better muscle development than if you perform just a single sport or exercise.

Is it true that training different muscle groups with cross training can improve your performance in a particular activity?
Because every exercise targets specific muscles, most experts believe there is no substitute for training in your own sport if you are a serious competitor. If you want to improve your running speed and endurance significantly, it is necessary to devote virtually all of your training time to running; the same applies to cycling, swimming or any other endurance sport. Some athletes believe that comparatively small amounts of cross training can supplement performance in their chosen sport; however, the most common reason single-sport athletes give for cross training is to maintain aerobic fitness while recovering from an injury. Cross training benefits, therefore, are actually best realized by triathletes, and by casual competitors and exercisers for whom exceptional performance in one particular sport or physical exercise is not the uppermost goal.

Why is a single aerobic exercise not sufficient for overall fitness?
As far as conditioning your heart is concerned, one aerobic exercise is adequate. The benefits that your cardiovascular system receives from any aerobic exercise are all-purpose: with training, your heart will pump a larger volume of blood with each contraction, your blood vessels will be better able to carry this increased supply, and more blood will go to the lungs, allowing more oxygenated blood to reach the muscles. This so-called training effect happens regardless of the kind of aerobic exercise you do.

However, exercise is very specific in what are called its peripheral effects, which are structural changes that enable muscles being exercised to use more oxygen to produce energy. The mitochondria — the energy factories within cells — increase in number and efficiency, the muscles develop more capillaries, so that more blood flows into them, and there are changes in the activity of enzymes that make the biochemical processes involved in metabolism more efficient. While any endurance exercise can improve cardiovascular conditioning, each activity works to develop different, specific sets of peripheral muscles.

So how do you gauge your level of fitness?
There is no single, precise measure of fitness. If you are well trained in a particular exercise, your VO_2max, which is a measure of how much oxygen your body can take in and process during one minute of intense activity, will be very high when you are performing that particular exercise. However, your VO_2max will be significantly lower when you perform a sport or exercise you have not trained for. Even though your heart and lungs are perfectly capable of taking in and delivering the same volume of oxygen, the untrained muscles that require the oxygen have a lower capacity to process it than trained muscles.

The limitations that peripheral muscles place upon measuring endurance is shown in several studies. For example, a group of subjects who rode stationary bicycles for eight weeks improved their VO_2max by 7.8 per cent — but when the subjects walked on a treadmill they showed only a 2.6 per cent improvement. In another study, 15 men trained intensively at swimming and raised their VO_2max by 11 per cent; when they were measured while running on a treadmill, they showed no improvement when compared with their pre-training rates. For this reason, VO_2max is not always the best way to measure a person's fitness. Another aspect of how well you can perform a particular endurance exercise is your anaerobic threshold, which has become an important component of training for endurance athletes.

What is the anaerobic threshold?
It is the point at which your body shifts from relying on aerobic metabolism — the oxygen-dependent energy system that sustains endurance exercise — to anaerobic metabolism, which supplies energy for short bursts of intense effort without using oxygen. Anaerobic

metabolism cannot be sustained for longer than a few minutes; therefore, raising your anaerobic threshold allows you to exert yourself more strenuously while still meeting your muscles' energy demands aerobically, so that you can continue a particular sport or activity for longer periods than before.

Anaerobic threshold is related to VO_2max, though the relationship for each person depends on his level of conditioning as well as the speed and duration of the exercise *(see chart, page 21)*. An untrained person might reach his anaerobic threshold at 50 per cent of his VO_2max, while a well-conditioned person might be able to exercise at 80 per cent of his VO_2max and still not reach his anaerobic threshold.

Researchers have charted this relationship by measuring the build-up of lactic acid, a chemical by-product of anaerobic metabolism that accumulates in the muscles and bloodstream and is associated with fatigue during exercise. Studies of trained and untrained subjects indicate that during light and moderate levels of exercise, the lactic acid level in the blood remains fairly constant for both groups. But as exercise becomes intense, untrained subjects exhibit a build-up of lactic acid sooner than trained subjects, whose lactic acid levels increase, but at a higher percentage of their VO_2max. Similarly, a high anaerobic threshold accounts for the superior performance capability of top-ranked endurance athletes, who can work more intensely — and therefore maintain higher speeds — than their less fit competitors without becoming exhausted.

The existence of the anaerobic threshold explains why a runner who is quite fit can quickly become exhausted when he starts swimming lengths or pedalling a bicycle; the lack of conditioning in the peripheral muscles permits more lactic acid to accumulate than running at the same oxygen cost would. In trying to increase your overall fitness, therefore, you should focus part of your training regimen on boosting your anaerobic threshold for a variety of activities — a strategy that need not involve more training time and that can make workouts more challenging.

How can you raise your anaerobic threshold?
Raising your anaerobic threshold depends on improving the conditioning of a particular type of skeletal muscle fibre. Skeletal muscles are made of two different types of fibres: fast twitch and slow twitch. Fast-twitch fibres, which contract rapidly, depend mostly on anaerobic metabolism for energy. Slow-twitch fibres, which contract at only about half the speed of the fast-twitch fibres, utilize energy that comes from aerobic metabolism.

When you walk or jog or perform other forms of light exercise, your nervous system recruits mainly the slow-twitch (also known as slow-oxidative) fibres to sustain this work. These capillary-rich fibres are slow to fatigue and so are well suited for endurance activities. If you concentrate on long slow distance training — when you exercise steadily at the low end of your target heart rate for a long time — you utilize the slow-twitch fibres. This kind of training will not raise your anaerobic threshold.

The larger but more easily fatigued fast-twitch fibres are called into use when you intensify your effort. These fast-twitch fibres can be further divided into two subsets: fast-oxidative-glycolytic (type A) and fast-glycolytic (type B). The type-A fibres are recruited when you pick up speed — going from jogging to running, for example — and the type-B fibres supply the surge of contractile power needed for sudden bursts of activity such as an all-out sprint. Type-A fibres must be exercised to raise your anaerobic threshold, since they utilize some aerobic as well as anaerobic energy; to exercise them, you must work close to but not above your anaerobic threshold. Research has shown that the closer you approach your anaerobic threshold when you work out, the more effectively you will be able to raise it. The chapters on swimming and cycling in this book include workouts to raise your anaerobic threshold, using interval training and sprints.

Can training change the proportion of your fast-twitch to slow-twitch muscle fibres?

This is unlikely. Although there is some evidence that your type-B fast-twitch fibres, which are dependent on anaerobic metabolism almost entirely, can be converted into type-A fast-twitch fibres with training, there is no evidence that fast-twitch fibres can become slow-twitch fibres, or vice versa.

There is a tremendous variation in the distribution of fibre types among individuals, and one person can even have different proportions from muscle to muscle. The average person has 45 to 50 per cent slow-twitch fibres, but the relative proportions of your fibre types are determined by heredity. Training can enhance the performance of both types of muscle fibres.

How much should you train?

The amount of training required to build and maintain cardiovascular fitness is well known: three weekly exercise sessions lasting a minimum of half an hour (including 20 minutes of activity at your target heart rate and five minutes each of warm-up and cool-down). How much you must train to build your peripheral conditioning, however, varies with the results you hope to achieve, how much time you can devote to exercise, and the condition you are in. A recent survey of triathletes found that while the serious competitor might train for several hours every day, most participants log in short distances frequently, scheduling their workouts to fit in with their daily lives.

In fact, most exercise physiologists now believe that the quality of your training matters more than the quantity. For example, swimmers have discovered that interval training, during which they swim relatively short distances with rest intervals in between each stretch, can

Despite the triathlon's "iron man" image, most people who enter triathlons do so for recreation, according to a recent survey of participants. The majority — 58 per cent — said they were swimming, cycling and running for fitness, while 33 per cent described their motivation as competition, and another 9 per cent were considering becoming competitive triathletes. The primary sports background of 52 per cent of all these athletes was running; 22 per cent were swimmers and 10 per cent were cyclists. Of the triathletes, 83 per cent were male, and their average age was 35. The female participants were slightly younger, at 32.

Anaerobic Threshold and Performance

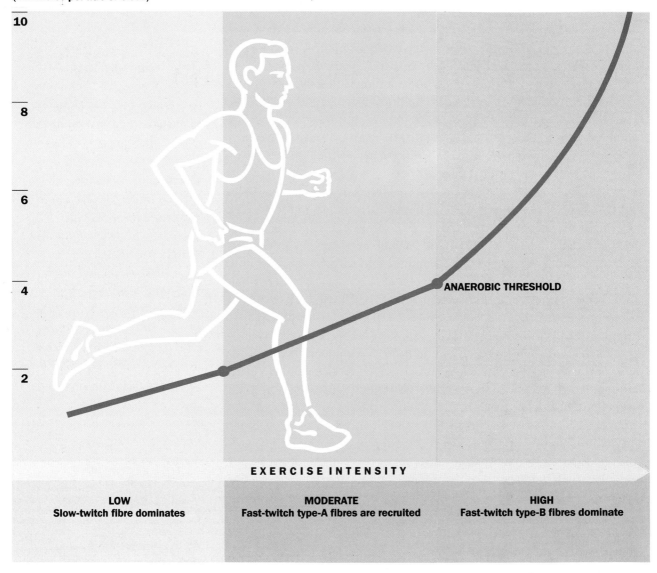

**Lactic acid
(millimoles per litre of blood)**

10

8

6

4 · ANAEROBIC THRESHOLD

2

EXERCISE INTENSITY

LOW	MODERATE	HIGH
Slow-twitch fibre dominates	Fast-twitch type-A fibres are recruited	Fast-twitch type-B fibres dominate

When exercise intensifies, your body's anaerobic system must meet the extra energy demand — a process that results in the production of lactic acid. The point at which lactic acid begins to build up in the bloodstream — followed quickly by fatigue — is called the anaerobic threshold. With training, you can raise the metabolic capacity of one type of fast-twitch fibre, which depends on anaerobic metabolism almost entirely. This will raise your anaerobic threshold, allowing you to increase your effort without fatigue.

build aerobic endurance faster than just swimming endless lengths at a slow, steady pace. (For information on interval training in swimming, see page 35.) Similarly, runners can use intervals to work on speed without exhausting themselves: running 1,600 metres (a mile) in four minutes is impossible for most people, but you can alternate running at this speed for 15 seconds at a time, with 30-second rest periods. If you train in this way for a total of 11 minutes and 30 seconds, you will accomplish the equivalent of 1,600 metres in four minutes.

How can you tell if you are overtraining?
Part of any good training programme is allowing adequate time for rest and recovery. Excessive training, and especially high-intensity

workouts day after day without periodic easy days, can be as much of a problem as insufficient training, paradoxically leading to increasingly poor performance and an actual loss of conditioning. Many well-motivated athletes encounter this problem, which occurs when the body's adaptive mechanisms have been stressed to the point of failure. There are a number of warning signals that may indicate overtraining: weight loss, joint and muscle pain in the absence of any injury, nausea, colds and constant fatigue. Women may also experience menstrual irregularities.

If you suspect that you might be overtraining, rest for a few days. In severe cases, a break of a week or more might even be necessary. When you return to your training programme, work out at a lower intensity or for a shorter time than you had been until you are certain that you have recuperated fully.

Is the ability to cross train limited by your age?

You can engage in endurance exercises regardless of your age. Active endurance athletes often reach their prime in their late twenties and early thirties — and many recreational exercisers and triathletes are older. The general rule in endurance sports is that the longer the event, the greater the edge older athletes may have, assuming that they are as well trained as the younger competitors. This edge depends on the older athletes' having trained consistently over the years. A recent survey of triathletes found that the average age of the men was 35, and of the women, 32.

Do you have to be an "iron man" to cross train?

Not any more. The phrase comes from the Hawaiian triathlon called the Ironman, which when staged initially in 1978 was the first major event of its kind. This race is aptly named: competitors swim 3.8 kilometres in open water, then cycle 180 kilometres, and finish with a 42-kilometre marathon. Today, with more and more people attracted to the sport, shorter triathlons far outnumber events as difficult as the Ironman. Chapter Four provides a training programme that will put you in shape for a short triathlon. Chapters Two and Three provide swimming and cycling techniques that can be applied to triathlon training, or to whichever type of cross training you perform. The following pages will guide you towards developing an effective, manageable training programme in swimming, cycling and running.

How much exercise is enough — and how much is too much? Scientists have calculated that expending 2,000 calories a week is the optimal rate for substantial fitness returns. This is equivalent to either running about 30 kilometres a week, cycling for five and a half hours or swimming for three hours. Increasing the amount of exercise can continue to provide physiological benefits, up to burning 6,000 calories per week; working out more than that, however, has not been proved to yield additional benefits.

How to Design Your Own Programme

Y ou do not need to adopt a rigorous regimen of cycling, swimming and running to cross train for fitness. A more casual programme, in which you supplement your primary fitness activity with an additional endurance sport, will also give you some of the benefits of cross training. Use the questions on the right to determine exactly which kind of cross training will suit you best.

Should you cross train?

1 **Are you bored or otherwise dissatisfied with your current exercise regimen?**

Even the most avid fitness enthusiasts can find that, after months or years of performing one activity, their routine becomes monotonous and their fitness gains reach a plateau. If this has happened to you, you may find challenges and new conditioning benefits by expanding your fitness programme to include one or more additional activities. You can incorporate cross training into your life informally — letting the seasons guide you, for example, by adding cross-country skiing in the winter, swimming in the summer or cycling in the autumn. Or you might decide to challenge yourself with a more rigorous programme in preparation for a triathlon.

2 **Are you fit enough for cross training?**

If you are just beginning a fitness regimen, you would be wise to stay with one sport until you are fairly well conditioned. Performing two (or more) types of exercise will stress more muscle groups, thereby contributing to additional muscle soreness until your body adapts. Also, it will take longer to master the skills involved in each activity if you constantly alternate between them. Get into shape by exercising in one sport three times a week, for half an hour per workout, and at a sufficient intensity to keep your heart in its target range for 20 minutes. Once you can do this comfortably, you can embark on a programme of cross training.

As your oxygen-delivery system improves, you can gradually start increasing the intensity and duration of your workouts — or you can add different activities. Bear in mind that you will not be able to perform a new exercise at the same intensity as the ones you have practised for a long time. Always proceed slowly, at a maximum weekly increase of 10 per cent more workout time or intensity. Going faster than this can place undue strain on your muscles, and this, in turn, can lead to injury.

3 **Have you suffered several exercise-related injuries in the past year?**

If you have had more than one injury serious enough to keep you from working out for several days at a time, it is possible that your current exercise routine is stressing your musculoskeletal system. This is especially true if your injuries tend to recur in the same areas — if you continually have problems with your knees, for example, of if you are repeatedly put out of action by shin splints.

Apart from acute injuries, such as a sprained ankle, most sports-related injuries are the result of an overuse syndrome that is due to repeated stress on one body part. Since different sports are powered by different muscle groups, you can reduce the incidence of overuse injuries by performing additional sports that strengthen previously undeveloped muscles. This will distribute the musculoskeletal stress more evenly throughout your body.

4 | Is one form of endurance exercise better than another?

The three most common activities used for cross training are swimming, running and cycling. Each sport makes specific demands on the musculoskeletal system and requires different skills. Swimming is the least demanding physiologically, because of both the cushioning effect of the water and your horizontal position in it — which makes it easier for your cardiovascular system to pump blood to the muscles. However, swimming is a most demanding activity in terms of technique. It can take several years for a non-swimmer to develop optimal technical skills — such as those demonstrated in Chapter Two — and neuromuscular co-ordination.

Running, by comparison, is a fairly simple activity to master, but the physiological effort of repeated pounding places great amounts of stress on your joints and muscles. Also, trainers have noticed that correcting runners' technical errors is more difficult than remedying swimmers' inefficient techniques. This may be because you learn to run as a child, so any problem with your technique is part of a long-established neurological pattern.

Cycling, demonstrated in Chapter Three, can be categorized between the two extremes: physiologically it is a less demanding activity than running, and it is less complex technically than swimming.

5 | How much time can you devote to training?

If you have an hour a day, four days a week, that you can devote to exercise, you can incorporate cross training into your life. You can simply alternate sports in a pattern of your own design. A more challenging training regimen that prepares you for a triathlon requires somewhat more time — up to 12.5 hours per week. Such a programme appears on pages 108-109.

Most coaches and athletes believe that the quality of training counts as much as the quantity. This means that you should experiment with shorter-distance intervals, hill work and drills, such as those shown in the following chapters. To guard against overtraining, always take one day off per week; rest is an integral part of any good training programme.

How hard should you work out?

The following chapters illustrate basic techniques for swimming and cycling that you can use for developing a well-rounded, varied programme in each activity. You can also use the charts on the following four pages to determine your training pace and to plan a regimen that raises your anaerobic threshold and builds endurance for long distance.

If you decide to challenge yourself by competing in a triathlon, you can use Chapter Four to help you prepare for it. Use the sample nine-week training programme on pages 108-109 to reach your personal best for triathlon competition.

Setting Your Pace

Whether you are cross training for a triathlon or for fitness alone, maximizing your training requires that you develop both your aerobic and your anaerobic capacities. Aerobic distance work, in which you exercise at 60 to 85 per cent of your VO_2max for at least 20 minutes, is your primary training emphasis. However, a good programme will also include anaerobic threshold training, and sprint or speed training, in which you work out at 75 to 90 per cent for anaerobic threshold training and 100 to 120 per cent of your VO_2max for sprint training.

To determine your proper pace range for the various modes of training, you should know your VO_2max. While laboratory testing is necessary for a precise determination of this figure, your maximum heart rate in an all-out time trial for the distances on the right will give your approximate heart rate at your VO_2max. The figure will be accurate to within plus or minus 5 per cent.

Perform the time trials for each sport on separate days after an adequate warm-up. Because the distances are comparatively short, you should sustain 100 per cent intensity for each trial. Immediately after you have finished, note the time elapsed and determine your heart rate; record both of these figures in the chart on the right — the second figure should be your maximum heart rate.

Use your time for each trial to determine your pace in the chart on the right. Then turn to pages 20-21 to correlate your VO_2max pace with the appropriate pace range for each activity. Every six weeks, perform another time trial in each event to assess your development; modify your training as your pace and your heart rate improve. (A strengthened, trained heart pumps a greater volume of blood with every contraction than an untrained heart. Therefore, you will find yourself needing to increase your training pace as your heart becomes stronger in order to reach your maximum heart rate.)

Your Personal Time Trial

	Distance	*Time*	*Heart rate/min.*	*Pace*
SWIMMING	**500 metres**	_____	_____	_____
CYCLING	**3 kilometres**	_____	_____	_____
RUNNING	**1,500 metres**	_____	_____	_____

Pace Chart

SWIMMING		CYCLING		RUNNING	
Total Time	**Min./100 m**	**Total Time**	**km/h**	**Total Time**	**Min./1,500 m**
11:15	2:15	9:00	20	10:30	10:30
10:25	2:05	8:11	22	9:30	9:30
9:35	1:55	7:30	24	8:30	8:30
8:45	1:45	6:55	26	7:30	7:30
7:55	1:35	6:25	28	7:15	7:15
7:05	1:25	6:00	30	7:00	7:00
6:40	1:20	5:37	32	6:45	6:45
6:15	1:15	5:17	34	6:30	6:30
5:50	1:10	5:00	36	6:15	6:15
5:25	1:05	4:44	38	6:00	6:00
5:00	1:00	4:30	40	5:45	5:45
		4:17	42	5:30	5:30
		4:05	44	5:15	5:15
		3:54	46	5:00	5:00
		3:45	48	4:45	4:45
		3:36	50	4:30	4:30

DISTANCE TRAINING
(60-85% VO_2max)

SWIMMING		CYCLING		RUNNING	
Time Trial Pace	Training Pace	Time Trial Pace	Training Pace	Time Trial Pace	Training Pace
Min./100 m		km/h		Min./1,500 m	
2:15	3:45-2:39	20	12.0-17.0	10:30	17:30-12:20
2:05	3:28-2:27	22	13.2-18.7	9:30	15:48-11:12
1:55	3:11-2:15	24	14.4-20.4	8:30	14:12-10:00
1:45	2:55-2:04	26	15.6-22.1	7:30	12:30-8:48
1:35	2:38-1:51	28	16.8-23.8	7:15	12:06-8:30
1:25	2:21-1:40	30	18.0-25.5	7:00	11:40-8:12
1:20	2:13-1:34	32	19.2-27.2	6:45	11:15-7:54
1:15	2:05-1:28	34	20.4-28.9	6:30	10:48-7:36
1:10	1:56-1:22	36	21.6-30.6	6:15	10:24-7:24
1:05	1:48-1:16	38	22.8-32.3	6:00	10:00-7:06
1:00	1:40-1:11	40	24.0-34.0	5:45	9:36-6:48
		42	25.2-35.7	5:30	9:12-6:30
		44	26.4-37.4	5:15	8:45-6:12
		46	27.6-39.1	5:00	8:20-5:54
		48	28.8-40.8	4:45	7:54-5:36
		50	30.0-42.5	4:30	7:30-5:18

ANAEROBIC THRESHOLD TRAINING
(75-90% VO_2max)

SWIMMING		CYCLING		RUNNING	
Time Trial Pace	Training Pace	Time Trial Pace	Training Pace	Time Trial Pace	Training Pace
Min./100 m		km/h		Min./1,500 m	
2:15	3:00-2:30	20	15.0-18.0	10:30	14:00-11:40
2:05	2:46-2:18	22	16.5-19.8	9:30	12:40-10:36
1:55	2:33-2:07	24	18.0-21.6	8:30	11:20-9:24
1:45	2:20-1:56	26	19.5-23.4	7:30	10:00-8:20
1:35	2:06-1:45	28	21.0-25.2	7:15	9:40-8:06
1:25	1:53-1:34	30	22.5-27.0	7:00	9:20-7:48
1:20	1:46-1:29	32	24.0-28.8	6:45	9:00-7:30
1:15	1:40-1:23	34	25.5-30.6	6:30	8:40-7:12
1:10	1:33-1:18	36	27.0-32.4	6:15	8:20-6:54
1:05	1:27-1:12	38	28.5-34.2	6:00	8:00-6:40
1:00	1:20-1:07	40	30.0-36.0	5:45	7:40-6:24
		42	31.5-37.8	5:30	7:20-6:06
		44	33.0-39.6	5:15	7:00-5:48
		46	34.5-41.4	5:00	6:40-5:36
		48	36.0-43.2	4:45	6:20-5:18
		50	37.5-45.0	4:30	6:00-5:00

SPRINT TRAINING
(100-120% VO_2max)

SWIMMING		CYCLING		RUNNING	
Time Trial Pace	Training Pace	Time Trial Pace	Training Pace	Time Trial Pace	Training Pace
Min./100 m		km/h		Min./1,500 m	
2:15	2:15-1:53	20	20.0-24.0	10:30	10:30-8:45
2:05	2:05-1:44	22	22.0-26.4	9:30	9:30-7:54
1:55	1:55-1:36	24	24.0-28.8	8:30	8:30-7:06
1:45	1:45-1:28	26	26.0-31.2	7:30	7:30-6:15
1:35	1:35-1:19	28	28.0-33.6	7:15	7:15-6:00
1:25	1:25-1:11	30	30.0-36.0	7:00	7:00-5:48
1:20	1:20-1:07	32	32.0-38.4	6:45	6:45-5:36
1:15	1:15-1:03	34	34.0-40.8	6:30	6:30-5:24
1:10	1:10-0:58	36	36.0-43.2	6:15	6:15-5:12
1:05	1:05-0:54	38	38.0-45.6	6:00	6:00-5:00
1:00	1:00-0:50	40	40.0-48.0	5:45	5:45-4:48
		42	42.0-50.4	5:30	5:30-4:36
		44	44.0-52.8	5:15	5:15-4:24
		46	46.0-55.2	5:00	5:00-4:12
		48	48.0-57.6	4:45	4:45-4:00
		50	50.0-60.0	4:30	4:30-3:45

Keeping Track

An accurate training log is, in essence, a progress report that can help you evaluate and improve your training and performance significantly. As shown in the diary on the right, which you can photocopy for repeated use, a log need not be complex. Simply keep a daily record of your training: the kind of workout — distance, anaerobic threshold or sprint — the amount of exercise and how long it took to complete. In addition, record in the final column how you felt about your workout at the time.

As important as these quantitative measures are, your comments on how you felt during the workout, both physically and psychologically, are equally vital for evaluating your programme's effectiveness. Were you tired? Were you coping with any injuries? Has your diet changed? Make a note of anything that might affect your progress, such as a cold or even a negative emotional reaction. Then use this information to measure how your training programme matches your needs, and if you should alter it.

WEEKLY TRAINING DIARY

Date		Distance Training	Anaerobic Threshold Training	Sprint Training	Comments
Su	SWIMMING				
	CYCLING				
	RUNNING				
M	SWIMMING				
	CYCLING				
	RUNNING				
Tu	SWIMMING				
	CYCLING				
	RUNNING				
W	SWIMMING				
	CYCLING				
	RUNNING				
Th	SWIMMING				
	CYCLING				
	RUNNING				
F	SWIMMING				
	CYCLING				
	RUNNING				
Sa	SWIMMING				
	CYCLING				
	RUNNING				

Weekly Totals

	Distance	Anaerobic	Sprint
SWIMMING	_____	_____	_____
CYCLING	_____	_____	_____
RUNNING	_____	_____	_____

One of the greatest benefits of cross training is that it allows you to develop more muscle groups than any single exercise can. For example, running develops your hamstrings primarily, while cycling focuses more on your quadriceps. By training in both of these sports, you will balance your overall muscle development.

However, such total body training means that your warm-ups have to be equally comprehensive. The stretches shown here and on the following six pages will enhance your flexibility in the muscles used for swimming, cycling and running. Even if you alternate workouts on different days, you should do the complete routine each time, since it will benefit muscle groups that complement one another, and so reduce the chance of injury.

Sit erect with your hands at your sides, your toes pointed and legs outstretched in front of you *(top)*. Slowly bend forwards from the waist, tucking your head and reaching for your ankles *(above)*. Hold for at least 30 seconds. Return to the starting position; repeat two or three times.

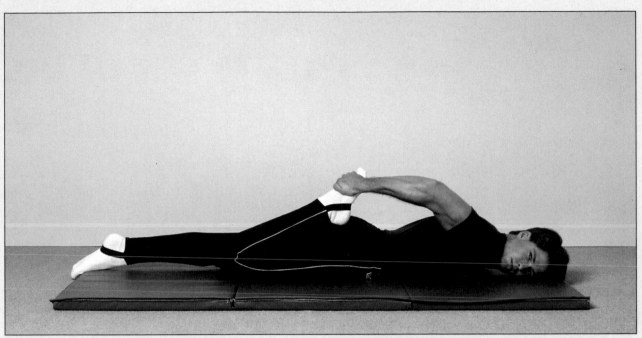

Lie flat on your stomach. Bend your right knee and reach behind you with your right arm, grasping your foot *(above)*. Hold for 30 seconds, lower and switch legs; repeat two or three times.

Sit with your left leg straight and your right leg crossed over it. Wrap your arms round your knee and pull it towards you *(above)*. Repeat two or three times; switch legs.

Sit with your back straight, your legs spread and your hands resting on the floor in front of you *(top)*. Slide your hands towards your feet as you bend forwards from the waist, leading with your chest *(above)*. Hold for 30 seconds; repeat two or three times.

From a sitting position, bend your knees and press the soles of your feet together. Grasp your ankles, and pull your feet towards you as far as possible *(above)*. Hold for 30 seconds; repeat two or three times.

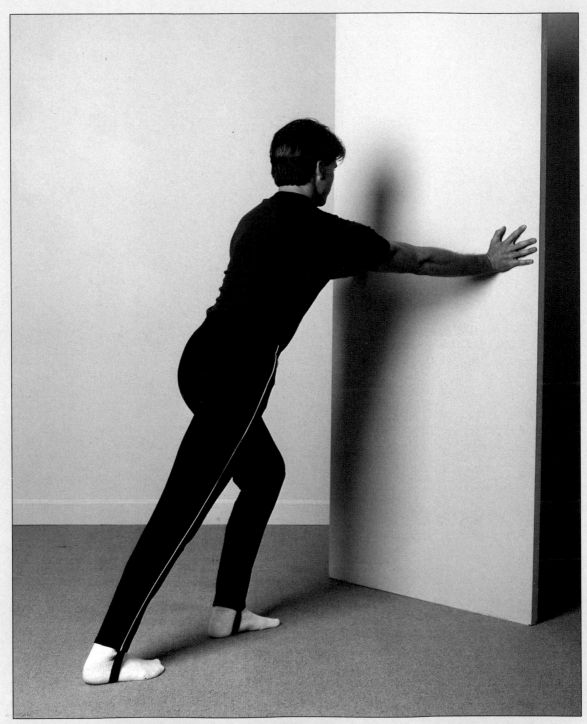

Stand in front of a wall at arm's length, and press your hands
against it at about shoulder height. Bend your left knee
forwards and stretch your right leg out behind you, pressing
both heels to the floor *(above)*. Lean your hips forwards slowly.
Hold for 30 seconds; switch legs; repeat two or three times.

Stand with your feet shoulder-width apart and your arms at your sides. Stretch your left arm up and over your head and bend to your right side *(above)*. Hold for 10 to 15 seconds. Return to the starting position; switch sides; repeat two or three times.

From a standing position, raise your right arm and bend it behind your head. Hold your right elbow with your left hand and pull it gently to the left *(above)*. Hold for 30 seconds; switch arms; repeat the entire sequence twice.

Conditioners/4

Lie flat on your stomach with your legs spread and your hands on the mat at your shoulders. Push your upper body off the mat, arching your back and neck and looking towards the ceiling *(above)*. Hold for five to 10 seconds. Return to the starting position; repeat two or three times.

Start in a sitting position with your legs outstretched and toes pointed. Clasp your hands behind your neck and bend forwards very gently, without pulling but stretching your neck as you reach your elbows to your thighs *(above)*. Hold for 10 to 30 seconds. Return slowly and repeat two or three times.

Lean forwards from a kneeling position and reach your left arm straight out to your right side. Place your right hand on top of your left, and stretch your upper body away from your hands to your left *(above)*. Hold for 30 seconds. Return to the starting position and repeat twice on each side.

From a kneeling position with your hands on the mat, extend your right arm out to your right side. Drop your head and right shoulder close to the mat, and stretch to your left *(above)*. You should feel the stretch in your chest. Hold for 30 seconds; switch sides; repeat twice.

CHAPTER TWO

Swimming

Strategies and drills for improving your speed, endurance and form

S wimming lengths is an excellent cardiovascular conditioner that builds both muscle strength and endurance with minimal risk of injury. Indeed, swimming is essentially the safest endurance activity because you perform it in the cushioning environment of water. However, length swimming — also called long slow distance swimming — has two potential drawbacks. First, going back and forth from one end of a pool to the other can be so boring that many swimmers quickly lose interest in the activity. Even more important, swimmers can become discouraged to find that after initial aerobic benefits, their rate of improvement in conditioning, speed and form begins to decline. Adding variety and intensity to your workouts by varying distances, incorporating drills and performing intervals is the best way to invigorate your swimming programme and improve your technique.

Distance workouts should form the base of any swimming programme. But once you have built an endurance foundation — that is, you can swim continuously for at least 20 minutes within your target heart rate — you can counter the boredom and diminishing returns of swimming lengths by varying your exercise programme. This is done with interval training — breaking your workout into shorter, faster swims that are interspersed with brief rest periods. (The box on the opposite page describes some of the different ways to employ intervals in your workout routines.)

A typical swimming programme that makes use of intervals consists of a slow warm-up swim, a period of interval training and a cool-down swim. Warm-ups generally account for 15 to 25 per cent of the total distance; cool-downs should be about 10 per cent. Longer warm-ups and cool-downs are advisable for particularly stressful workouts. Another 30 per cent of each workout can be devoted to the technical aspects of stroking, kicking and breathing drills, such as those shown on pages 41, 46-47, and 50-51.

One of the best ways to improve a swimming routine is to concentrate each workout on a particular level of effort. The ratios of work intensity or speed, duration and recovery time determine just how aerobic or anaerobic an interval is. A well-rounded swimming programme includes short, maximum-effort swims to develop sprinting ability and technique; middle-distance workouts to improve lactic acid tolerance and to increase your anaerobic threshold; and distance work to build endurance, concentration and a sense of pacing. The length of your rest period and level of effort used determine whether sprinting ability or lactic acid tolerance is being emphasized in the workout: the farther your heart rate drops between swim repeats (the distance you swim without resting), the more your workout emphasizes speed instead of endurance.

In a distance "set", or series of lengths, you swim continuously for up to 2,000 metres, or more, with rest periods taking only 20 to 25 per cent of the total workout time. The object of a programme of this kind — often called an overdistance workout because you swim "over" the distance of most races — is to maintain an elevated heart rate and a steady pace for relatively long periods.

Shorter repeats of less than 200 metres, performed fast enough for your muscles to use anaerobic energy, are typical of middle-distance swimming. Because your pace is faster than it would be in an overdistance workout, you require more substantial periods of rest between swims. A typical middle-distance swim would consist of 200 metres at an easy pace, followed by a 30-second rest, then 200 metres at a faster pace, followed by a 20-second rest, and a final 200 metres at your fastest pace.

While the main goal of sprint training is to increase your speed, it also enhances stroke efficiency by improving the neuromuscular coordination of your swimming. Even if you do not want to become the fastest swimmer in your pool, you can enhance your technique by including sprint swims in your workout. Short, fast swims that raise your heart rate quickly to or above your target zone build

Interval Training

◆ When you perform intervals, each distance you swim without stopping is called a repeat; groups of repeats are called sets. For example, if you were to swim repeats of 100 metres in a 25-metre pool, you would swim the length of the pool four times without a rest for each repeat.

◆ Intervals are expressed as the number of swims times the lengths of the swim times the amount of time between departures. You might, for instance, decide to swim 10 x 100 x 1:50, which would mean swimming 10 repeats of 100 metres, beginning each swim 1 minute and 50 seconds after the previous one. The faster you swim each set, the longer you can rest during each interval.

◆ You can swim decreasing interval sets, in which you shorten the interval for each swim. For example, you could swim your first three of 10 swims in 1 minute and 50 seconds, the next three in 1:40 and the next in 1:20. You could follow this last group with an extra long rest and then swim the last repeat as fast as you possibly can.

◆ Another alternative is swimming ladder sets, in which you vary the distances of the repeats. For example, you could swim 50, 100, 150, 200, 250 and 300 metres in a set of six. To calculate the interval for each repeat, you can use a constant rest interval — of 30 seconds, for instance — between every interval swim.

sprinting ability. Because moving very quickly into this high-performance zone is stressful, you must take relatively long rests between sprints at first, with the rest periods lasting considerably longer than the swim times. A typical sprint lasts less than 10 seconds; a typical rest lasts at least twice that long. The distance you swim for this type of training should be between 15 and 100 metres.

Incorporating these various strategies into a typical week of training, you might include one session of distance training, two or three sessions of middle-distance training and a session or two of sprinting, alternating the workouts to minimize boredom. For most swimmers, it is a good idea to establish technique and endurance before working on speed. Paying attention to your technique is especially important because minor lapses in swimming form are common, even among experienced swimmers, and such mistakes can be more costly than faults in running or cycling technique, since the resistance of water is so much greater than wind resistance. The following pages not only demonstrate the most efficient form for performing the front crawl, or freestyle, swimming stroke — the stroke most often used for endurance swimming — but also show you the mistakes that swimmers are most likely to make. You will also find drills to help you perfect your form. Work on some aspects of your form during every workout; this helps to make the exercise more challenging, and you will be rewarded with small but steady improvements.

Streamlining

The hydrodynamics of swimming are based on principles similar to the aerodynamics of flying: an object that is flatter and more streamlined will move through either water or air faster than an angled object, which catches more resistance. A flat, streamlined swimming position creates relatively little disruption of the water. This means that the swimmer will encounter less resistance — called drag — to hold him back, and require less energy for forward momentum.

Proper body alignment, shown on these two pages, is probably the most essential element of good swimming form, since effective stroke mechanics, kicking form and breathing techniques all stem from it. Your body should be streamlined both horizontally and laterally. Horizontal streamlining will keep you flat and shallow in the water so that you encounter minimum resistance to forward motion. Aligning your body laterally will keep it in a straight line so that it does not fishtail from side to side, which increases resistance by presenting a greater body area to the water. (In this chapter, common mistakes in body position, stroking and other aspects of form are shown in black-and-white photographs.)

For lateral streamlining, your head, shoulders, hips and feet should be aligned *(above)*. When stroking, your body should twist as a unit; avoid side-to-side swaying. Kicking helps to counterbalance the rolling caused by your arm stroke.

To streamline your body horizontally, keep it as flat as possible in the water. Your head should be lowered so it breaks the water at about your hairline; your back should be level and your feet and legs near the water's surface *(above)*.

WRONG Inclining your body at a diagonal to the water's surface *(right)* leads to inefficient swimming. Your hips and legs are sunken at a downward angle, while your head is high, which increases lateral resistance as you swim.

Stroking Mechanics

Most of your momentum in swimming will come from your stroke. On these and the following 10 pages, the crawl, or freestyle, stroke — the stroke most frequently used by both fitness and competitive swimmers — is broken into its component parts and accompanied by examples of typical errors and corrective drills. Taking time to learn the elements of your stroke and to analyse it will improve your swimming efficiency markedly.

The freestyle stroke can be divided into three phases, starting with the entry phase — the beginning of the stroke in which the hand first enters the water. This phase ends with the catch, when the hand, now underwater, first applies pressure to the water. The power phase, which includes the pull, push and finish, shown on pages 42-47, actually moves the water backwards to provide the stroke's forward momentum. Finally, in the recovery phase, demonstrated on pages 48-49, the hand and arm leave the water behind you and then circle forwards through the air to prepare for the next stroke cycle.

Although the three stroke phases are examined independently, it is important to remember that they are interrelated: effective stroking is contingent on both a proper entry and a proper recovery. You will most enhance your swimming by perfecting all areas of stroking.

ENTRY The point at which your hand enters the water should be in line with your ear and between 20 and 30 centimetres in front of your head. While your hand is still out of the water, hold your elbow high and bent at an angle of almost 90 degrees. Keep your palm pitched, or tilted, outwards at a 45-degree angle so that your thumb enters the water first *(above)*.

As this underwater view of the entry shows, your hand should lead, with your bent elbow following *(top)*. In a correct entry, the pitch of the hand will allow a minimum of drag-creating bubbles. To prepare for the catch of the entry *(above)*, as you enter the water, extend your elbow and press your hand forwards, elevating your shoulder girdle as you push downwards gradually to about 30 centimetres below the water's surface.

Entry Errors and Drills

WRONG A typical entry mistake is to extend your arm before it enters the water *(right)*. This not only strains the muscles of the shoulder and the back, but also traps air bubbles, creates more drag and can hinder proper torso rotation.

WRONG Reaching past the body's centre line *(left)* disrupts your lateral alignment by causing your hips and shoulders to turn from side to side excessively. Your arm should not cross in front of your head on entry.

DRILL Exaggerating the point of entry will allow you to both feel and visualize the difference between proper entry and either overextending or overreaching. Instead of entering with your arm about 30 centimetres in front of your head, bend your elbow more sharply and push your hand downwards into the water like a piston, right next to your ear *(above)*. Alternate one length of drill swimming with one length of ordinary swimming for five to ten 25-metre laps.

The Power
Phase/1

During this part of the stroke, your arm
sweeps from the catch position in front
of your body to the finish behind you. The
force of the power phase is determined
largely by the roll of your shoulders and
torso, which should rotate upwards about
45 degrees as your arm moves past.

1

2

3

4

The power phase of the stroke starts with the pull (1), during which you push your hand downwards, turning it in towards the centre line of your body, and start to bend your elbow. As the pull continues (2), flex your wrist and continue bending your elbow until it reaches a maximum angle of about 90 degrees when your arm is beneath your chest. At this point, begin the push phase (3), by rotating your hand to face almost directly behind you as it pushes the water away. Finally, at the finish (4), begin to straighten your elbow as it leaves the water, rotating your palm in towards your thigh as your hand continues to push backwards. Your little finger should lead as your hand begins to leave the water. When performing the power phase correctly, you should feel constant pressure on your palms.

The Power Phase/2

The correct elbow bend during the power phase *(right)* is crucial if you are to achieve maximum propulsion while swimming. Ideally, you should start bending your elbow immediately after the catch, and it should reach a maximum bend of 90 degrees when it is directly beneath your body. The angle of your elbow should gradually increase as you continue to push backwards.

WRONG The dropped elbow *(right)* is the most serious of all stroking flaws: the elbow is prematurely bent so that it is lower than the hand when entering the water. This wastes energy, since the lowered elbow and shoulder are not in a maximum power position and so cannot move the water effectively. In addition, this incorrect position can lead to shoulder injuries.

WRONG Powering your stroke with a straight elbow *(right)* is also ineffective, since it relies strictly on arm strength for power, and does not allow you to utilize the larger and stronger muscles of your back. This stroking flaw can also decrease torso rotation and lead to shoulder injuries.

Power Drills

Swimming on your side is a good way to practise the correct rotation of your torso which will enhance the power phase of your stroke. After completing a normal left-arm stroke cycle, turn on to your right side, extending your right arm underneath your body, and kick 10 times *(right)*. Return to a horizontal position and complete another full stroke cycle, then turn on to your left side and repeat *(below)*. Perform this for 25 metres.

A pulling set that works on the propulsive power of your stroke should comprise 10 to 20 per cent of your workout. Use flotation devices to keep your legs suspended at the correct height *(above)*, so that all of your momentum comes from your upper body. Insert a buoyancy aid between your upper thighs and, if you like, secure your ankles inside a small inner tube.

Recovery

A good recovery provides your arm with a restful transition between the more propulsive entry and power phases. Your elbow should emerge from the water first, with your forearm perpendicular to it (1). Increase your elbow bend as you bring your hand fully out of the water and up along your side (2). Start to extend your forearm, bringing your hand forwards in front of your head (3). Finally, swing your whole arm forwards as you prepare for another entry phase into the water (4).

3   4

WRONG A wide recovery is a common stroking error in which the arm stays straight and swings outwards in a wide arc *(right)*. This can disrupt lateral streamlining, causing you to lose energy. Be sure that your elbow exits the water before your hand, and that it stays bent through the entire recovery.

WRONG The palm of your hand should not show during the recovery *(right)*. The recovery phase should give your arm a chance to relax, and rotating your hand outwards creates stress that can cause shoulder injuries.

The Flutter Kick

While the forward momentum of swimming comes almost entirely from the stroking action of your arms, the kick has a crucial function: it prevents your lower body from sinking, helping to maintain streamlining.

The two most typical kick styles are the two-beat and six-beat kicks. In a two-beat kick, the swimmer kicks once with each arm stroke; in the six-beat kick, three times per arm stroke. Generally, two-beat kicks plunge a little deeper than the more rapid six-beat kick. There are also less common kick variations, such as the four-beat kick — two kicks per arm stroke — and the two-beat crossover in which the feet actually scissor across each other. Ideally, you will develop your own kicking rhythm after you have perfected your stroke. The kick that you use is largely — and best — determined by your particular body mechanics and by your stroking style.

Whichever beat kick you use, your form should be the same. Keep your toes pointed and your knees almost straight. The kicking action should come from your hips. Your feet should be about 30 centimetres apart at the widest point. Do not actually bring your upper foot out of the water completely; rather, your heel should just break the water's surface.

WRONG The hooked foot *(above)*, with ankles flexed and toes pointed straight downwards, decreases the effectiveness of your kick. Because it is less streamlined, this kicking flaw drags your lower body downwards and wastes energy.

Kicking Drills

Using a kickboard is one of the best ways to perfect your kick as well as to condition your leg muscles. Stretch the board in front of you fully and grasp it on either side just where it begins to round *(left)*. Keep your body aligned, with your shoulders low and your hips near the water's surface. Spend 10 to 15 per cent of your workout on kicking drills.

Another way to practise kicking is on your side. Your lower arm should be fully extended to keep your body up. Power the kick from your hips. Perform this for 25 metres on your left side; repeat the drill on your right side.

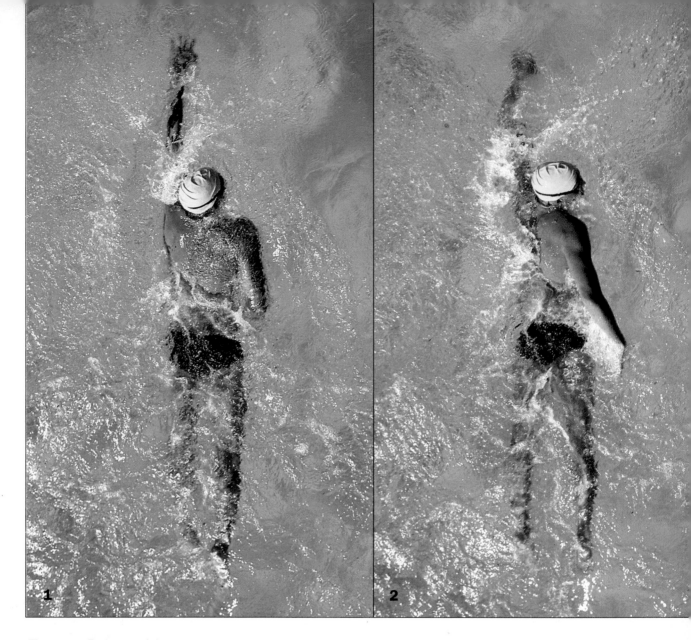

1

2

Breathing/1

Rhythmic, relaxed breathing is essential to swimming, as it prevents fatigue and aids in stroke mechanics. It should require no more thought than breathing while doing any other physical activity. Quite simply, you should exhale completely through both your mouth and your nose while your face is under water, and inhale through your mouth when your arm begins its recovery. One breath intake per stroke cycle — a right and left arm stroke — is usually adequate for most swimmers.

Determining which side to breathe on is a matter of personal preference, and many experts believe that swimmers should be able to breathe bilaterally, as demonstrated here. Whichever side you breathe on, turn your head into the trough of water, or bow wave, created by your head during forward momentum. The gap created by the bow wave will allow you more time to inhale.

When breathing bilaterally, take a breath every third arm stroke: as your right arm begins its recovery, take advantage of your body's rolling movement and start turning your neck to the right (1). When your right arm first leaves the water, turn your head fully to inhale (2). Roll your head back to the centre line of your body and exhale as your right arm completes its recovery (3). Keep your head submerged and exhale gradually during a complete left and right-stroke cycle, then inhale to your left as you begin your recovery (4).

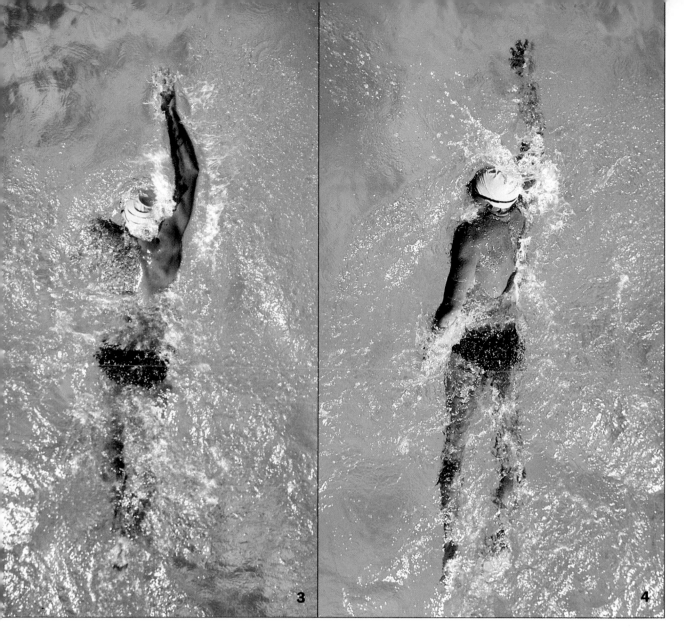

3

4

WRONG Breathing late in the recovery, or turning your head too far underneath your arm, causes your torso to twist out of lateral alignment, reducing stroke efficiency *(above)*. Avoid this by starting to turn your head as your arm begins its recovery.

Breathing/2

The correct head position assists in breathing and also ensures that optimal streamlining is maintained. When exhaling, your head should be half submerged and your eyes focused downwards at an angle of about 45 degrees *(left)*. As your arm completes its pull and begins its recovery, turn your head to follow the natural roll of your body *(below)*, but continue rotating your neck to allow your mouth and nose to emerge from the water for inhaling.

Strengtheners for Swimmers/1

While swimming primarily strengthens the muscles of the upper body, it does entail some use of all the body's major muscle groups. Conditioning these muscles through specific strengthening exercises will allow you to develop more power in both your stroke and your kick, and to use them more effectively. As a result, you will be able to swim farther and faster without fatigue.

The swim strengtheners that are demonstrated here and on the following four pages concentrate on the muscles of the shoulders, the legs and the abdomen. They are designed to strengthen the primary as well as secondary muscle groups required for swimming. Some of the exercises require weights. Start by using 1 or 1.5-kilogram dumbbells or ankle weights. As your strength improves, you can increase the weight.

Holding dumbbells, stand straight with your feet together and arms at your side. Raise your arms out to your sides at shoulder height (1); lower (2). Raise your arms to shoulder height in front of you (3); lower; perform eight to 15 repetitions.

Place your bent right knee and straight right arm on a weight bench, keeping your back flat. Hold a dumbbell in your left hand and let your arm dangle *(below, left)*. Bend your elbow and raise the dumbbell to the side of your torso *(below)*; lower; perform eight to 15 repetitions; switch arms.

Sit erect with your hands at your sides, your right knee bent and your left leg extended in front of you. Raise your left leg from 10 to 30 centimetres off the mat *(above)*; hold momentarily, then lower slowly. Perform 10 to 20 repetitions; switch legs.

Lie on your back with your right knee bent and your left leg extended. Place your hands on your hips and raise your left leg until it is perpendicular to the floor, keeping your knee bent *(above)*. Lower slowly. Repeat 10 to 20 times; switch legs.

Lie face down with your legs extended and your elbows bent at shoulder level. Keeping your toes pointed, tighten your buttocks while raising your right leg high, without arching your back *(above)*; hold for two seconds and lower slowly. Repeat 10 to 20 times; switch legs.

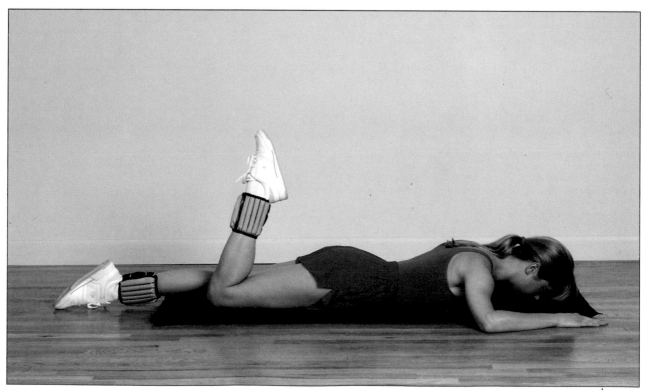

Wear ankle weights and lie face down on a mat with your elbows bent at shoulder level. Bend your right knee and raise your calf, keeping your toes pointed *(above)*. Lower slowly; repeat 10 to 20 times; switch legs.

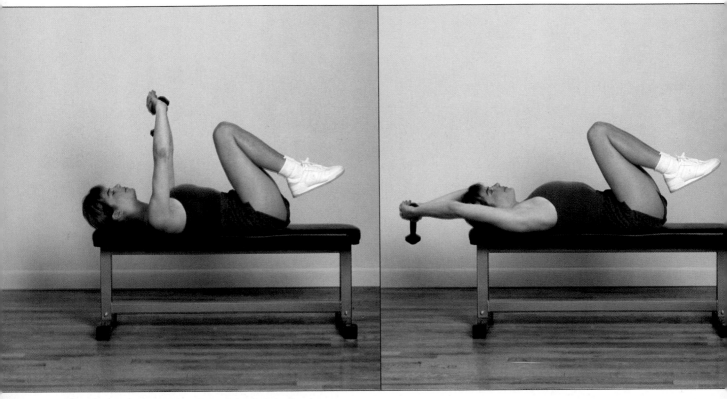

Lie on a weight bench with your knees bent, thighs pulled towards your torso and lower back flat. Hold a dumbbell between two hands above your chest with your arms extended and elbows slightly bent *(above)*. Stretch your arms over your head, letting the weight hang downwards *(above, right)*. Return to the starting position; repeat eight to 15 times.

Lie on your back with your knees bent and feet flat on the floor, and your arms crossed over your chest *(top)*. Using your abdominals, raise your head, shoulders and upper back *(above)*. Hold momentarily; lower slowly and repeat 10 to 30 times.

CHAPTER THREE

Cycling

*Outdoor conditioning
on varied terrain*

Cyclists are far more dependent on equipment than are runners or swimmers. Yet, in a sense, cycling is the freest and most versatile of exercises. You can move with speed, outdoors, on a machine that not only transports you, but is powered by you; you can cover the sweeping distances and the varied terrain that you might travel in a car; and you can enjoy this blend of body and machine in a variety of circumstances — cycling on scenic tours alone or with a group, commuting to work, unwinding with a ride at the end of the day, or competing in races.

If you are already an experienced cyclist, you are probably aware of some of the benefits of this sport. Bicycle riding not only tones and strengthens your legs and shoulders, but also helps stretch your lower back, conditioning it for swimming and running. For injured runners, cycling is ideal, since it exercises the leg muscles while imposing far less stress than running. In terms of developing aerobic capacity, cycling can be as effective as running.

In the past few years, the introduction of mountain bikes — also known as all-terrain bikes or ATBs — has extended the enjoyment of biking by letting cyclists traverse trails and slopes that were once inaccessible to them. Because these bikes allow better manoeuvrability and a more upright position than racing or touring bicycles (*see page 92*), many bicycle commuters have adopted ATBs for city riding.

If you do not have a bicycle, the information on pages 68-69 provides guidelines for choosing one, and explains the major differences between a 10 or 12-speed racing or touring bike, and an ATB. Just as important as choosing a bike is fitting it to your dimensions. In a study at the U.S. Olympic Training Center, racing cyclists increased their cardiovascular efficiency by 8 to 14 per cent simply by having their bicycles fitted properly — an effect equivalent to losing almost 5 kilograms of body weight (*see the box on the opposite page*).

Having a bike that fits you properly is the first step towards feeling comfortable on it; learning to handle it confidently is the next. Indeed, cyclists training for Olympic competition are so relaxed that they can graze one another without falling when they are in the middle of a pack moving at 40 kilometres per hour. The point of such mastery is not simply to avoid falls, but also to feel at ease so that your energy for forward propulsion is conserved. The riding techniques shown on the following pages are designed to help keep your upper body and torso movement to a minimum and let your legs do the work.

Because a bicycle is such an efficient machine, it is possible to go for a ride and never reach your target heart rate. If your cardiovascular system is already well conditioned from another aerobic activity, familiarize yourself with cycling by riding on relatively flat terrain for 20 to 30 minutes three times a week for at least two weeks. Begin each ride by pedalling in a low gear at a steady 55 to 60 revolutions per minute to warm up; after 10 minutes, increase your cadence to 70 to 80 rpms and change to a low or medium gear that raises your heart rate into its training zone. Perhaps the most common mistake that novice cyclists make is to pedal in too high a gear, which will not only wear you out quickly, but will put undue strain on your knees. Use this initial period to concentrate on high-rpm, low-gear riding and to improve your bike-handling skills.

Over the next two to four weeks, add a fourth cycling day per week and climb some modest hills twice weekly. Try to accomplish a minimum of three rides of 45 to 60 minutes; use weekends for at least one longer, relatively easy ride of 30 to 45 kilometres. After five or six weeks, your technique should improve considerably and your cadence should be a steady 75 to 90 rpms.

With this conditioning as a base, you should reach the point in your third month of training when you can ride 45 to 65 kilometres at a time, and be able to increase your weekly distance by 8 to 10 per cent. Add variety to your cycling programme by climbing steeper hills or by interval training. Your aim should be to increase your heart rate to 80

Fitting Your Bike

For optimal cycling efficiency and comfort, it is crucial that your bike be fitted properly to your body proportions. If you purchase a new bike at a reputable bike shop, the sales staff will help you take the proper measurements and make any adjustments. However, with the help of a friend, it is simple to determine the correct size for you by using the following guidelines. (The diagrams on pages 68-69 identify the parts of a bicycle that are referred to below.)

◆ Your first consideration is the frame size itself, which cannot be adjusted. You should know this measurement when you begin examining a bike to make a purchase. Hold the handlebars steady and straddle the top tube so that you are standing flat-footed on the ground in front of the saddle. There should be a 3 to 5-centimetre clearance between the top tube and your crotch. Because a smaller frame size is preferable on an ATB, you should allow a clearance of 5 to 7 centimetres.

◆ To determine the appropriate saddle height, ask someone to hold the handlebars steady while you sit in a comfortable riding position with your hands on the handlebars. When the pedal is at its lowest point, in the six o'clock position, your knee should be slightly bent.

◆ Assessing how far to slide the saddle forwards or backwards requires the use of a plumb line. Sit in a comfortable riding posture while someone holds the bike steady. Place the pedals at the three o'clock/nine o'clock position. A plumb line held directly behind your kneecap should fall straight past the ball of your foot and down to the pedal axle.

◆ To adjust the height of the handlebars and stem, ask someone to hold you steady while you sit on the saddle. Position the bars and stem about 3 to 5 centimetres below the bottom of the saddle. For correct stem length, hold one of your elbows against the tip of the saddle, and extend your forearm straight forwards towards the stem. Your middle finger should reach half way across the length of the stem.

per cent of its maximum for three to five-minute intervals, followed by rest periods during which you pedal easily in a low gear for five minutes. Repeat this sequence four or five times. Vary the length and intensity of riding intervals, depending on how you feel, but do not overdo them; experienced cyclists generally limit bouts of interval training to twice a week. Mountain biking also provides an ideal opportunity for intervals of intense riding, since trekking over uneven trails makes you work harder than riding over metalled roads.

After three months of building your overall stamina, you will be ready to train for specific events, with their different requirements. Riding a century — a 100-mile (160-kilometre) ride — calls for increasing your weekly training to at least 225 kilometres and being able to do two five or six-hour rides on successive days. For bicycle touring, it is helpful to devote at least two days a week to hill climbing, and also to condition your upper body to handle a bike loaded with packs weighing as much as 15 to 20 kilograms. Whatever your biking goals are, you will benefit from learning the riding techniques and conditioning exercises in this chapter.

The Right Bike

ROAD BIKE

DROP HANDLEBARS

HEAD TUBE

BRAKE HOOD

BRAKE LEVER

FRONT BRAKE

FORK

QUICK RELEASE

RIM

BRAKE CABLE

STEM

GEAR LEVER

DOWN TUBE

TOP TUBE

SADDLE

SEATPOST

SEATPOST BINDER BOLT

REAR BRAKE

SEAT TUBE

FREEWHEEL

REAR DERAILLEUR

CHAINSTAY

FRONT DERAILLEUR

CHAINRING

CRANKARM

TOE CLIP

PEDAL

SEATPOST QUICK RELEASE

WIDER SADDLE

LARGE-DIAMETER TUBING

UPRIGHT HANDLEBARS

GEAR LEVER

CANTILEVER BRAKE

KNOBBY TYRE

NUTTED OR
QUICK-RELEASE
AXLE

SMALLER FRAME SIZE
THAN COMPARABLE
ROAD BIKES

PEDAL WITH
SOLE GRIPS

LONGER
CRANKARM

TRIPLE CHAINRING

U-BRAKE OR
ROLLER CAM

VARIABLE-LENGTH
CHAINSTAY

LONG-CAGE DERAILLEUR

WIDE-RANGE
FREEWHEEL

ALL—TERRAIN BIKE

B uying a good bicycle is an investment. If you are to choose wisely, you must be familiar with bike parts and the differences between road or touring and all-terrain bicycles (*above*).

The most apparent differences between these two popular types of bicycles are the smaller, heavier frame sizes, upright handlebars and wider, knobby tyres of the ATBs. While these features increase your riding stability and comfort, they also result in less speed potential. The cantilever brakes, U-brakes or roller cams found on ATBs are bigger and more powerful than the brakes on road bikes.

ATBs also provide up to 18 gears, which allow you more options and control when climbing steep hills or navigating over rough terrain. Such features are not needed on a road bike used for touring or racing.

The Right Equipment

Bicycle equipment for the dedicated cyclist does not end with the purchase of the bike itself. Having the right cycling accessories can improve your performance as well as increase your riding comfort and safety.

Clockwise from the top right, a good helmet is a necessity; it will greatly reduce your risk of injury in the event of a fall. Helmets must pass nationwide safety standards established by the British Standards Institute (BSI); be sure you choose one with a BSI approval sticker. Today's helmets come both in hard-shell construction and as lighter, Styrofoam models, weighing about 200 grams.

Saddles can be purchased separately to suit your particular riding needs. Gel-filled saddles increase riding comfort greatly by providing additional form-fitting cushioning. A cyclometer, which clips on your handlebars and measures distance, cadence and time, is a valuable training aid. A water bottle, which attaches to a holder on the bike's downtube, is another essential.

Padded cycling gloves protect your hands from blisters and minimize road shock. Similarly, well-padded cycling shorts have a deerskin or synthetic-lined crotch that absorbs moisture and protects your inner thighs and groin from chafing and saddle sores.

Cycling shoes feature inflexible soles that increase your pedalling efficiency. Experienced riders choose cleated shoes or the latest pedal/shoe systems, where the shoes clip on to the pedals directly.

The correct cycling posture shown here demonstrates the importance of streamlining. Lower your torso by bending forwards at the waist, keeping your back parallel to the top tube *(right)*. Your head should be low, with your neck in line with your spine. Keep your elbows flexed slightly and tucked towards your knees.

Body Position

Your position on a bicycle can make a considerable difference in both the effectiveness and the comfort of your riding. One study that examined the effects of several variables on speed showed that improved riding position, with a time decrease of four minutes and 31 seconds, accounted for a greater benefit than any other variable.

Proper riding posture begins with an accurate fit of the bike to your body *(page 67)*. Only after such adjustments are made can you evaluate your actual riding posture.

To achieve an optimal cycling position, consider two dynamics. First, distribute your body weight between the handlebars and the saddle. Weight distribution is dictated by terrain, and can be adjusted by changing your hand positions *(pages 74-75)* as well as sliding backwards or forwards on the saddle. Second,

minimize wind resistance. Research has shown that 90 per cent of your cycling energy is expended in pushing air away from you. Thus, the more you streamline your body position by keeping your torso as horizontal as possible, the more effective your riding will be: you will not only meet much less resistance when you are riding against the wind, but also pick up more speed when riding with it.

Hand Positions

Hold the handlebars near the stem when hill climbing from a seated position or for a rapid, smooth descent with no braking required to slow down.

Resting your hands on the handlebars above the brake levers is ideal for cruising, since it allows you to assume a slightly more upright, relaxed posture.

Grasping the brake hoods provides easy access to the brakes for riding downhill. In this position, you can lightly stroke the brakes off and on with your first two fingers.

Wrap your hands round the tops of the brake levers to shift your body weight to the front of the bike for making out-of-the-saddle uphill climbs.

Place your hands in the dropped part of the handlebars below the brake hoods, which allows easy access to the brake levers, for rapid descents that might require braking.

You will frequently need to ride with only one hand on the handlebars, whether to change gears or to take something to eat from your shirt pocket. Stabilize the bike by moving both hands close to the handlebar stem; then you can steer safely with one hand without losing your balance.

Maintaining a straight line while turning to look behind you is a simple — but necessary — skill, especially when riding in traffic. Keeping your hands close to the handlebar stem, maintain a straight line by turning your head only, with the weight of your body centred forwards.

For efficient pedalling, both legs should be in constant motion of equal effort, with your knees tucked in close to the bike *(above)*. When one foot is at the 12 o'clock position to begin the downstroke, the other is about to begin the upstroke from the six o'clock position *(top left)*. The 12-to-six o'clock downstroke utilizes your quadriceps and anterior lower leg muscles; the six-to-12 o'clock upstroke works the hamstrings and calf group of muscles.

Pedalling

Skilful pedalling is probably the most important aspect of cycling. New cyclists often think of pedalling as an up-and-down motion — an ineffective way to ride, since it will overdevelop some muscles of the leg while under-utilizing others. Instead, pedal in a smooth, circular pattern to distribute the workload throughout the leg muscles. This depends as much on pulling upwards on the pedals as it does on pushing downwards.

To perform smooth rotations, and make sure that your upward and downward force on the pedals is equal, it is essential that your bike be equipped with toe clips, or that you have cleated shoes that lock into the pedals. Practise inserting your feet in and taking them out of the toe clips so that you are prepared to disengage them if you need to stop.

For maximum cycling speed and endurance, your cadence, or pedalling rhythm, should be constant. Cadence is measured in revolutions per minute, or rpms. Strive to pedal between 80 and 90 rpms; with practise, this cadence will become second nature. To determine your cadence, count the complete pedal strokes of one foot for 15 seconds and multiply this number by four.

One-legged pedalling will isolate the pedalling action to strengthen your hip flexors, and thus improve your upstroke. To perform this exercise, put your bike on a windloader, or home trainer, such as the one shown on the right. This valuable training aid — available at most cycle or sports-equipment shops — holds your rear wheel upright and stationary, allowing you to pedal at a particular resistance or rpm. Pedal for 10 minutes for each leg at a constant cadence, extending your resting leg to the side.

MEDIUM GEAR

CHANGE TO HIGHER GEAR

CHANGE TO LOWER GEAR

Gearing

Gearing is an indispensable element of efficient pedalling, since it enables you to maintain a constant cadence over different types of ground. Efficient gearing depends on the incline and condition of the road. Adjust your gears whenever your cadence drops or increases for more than a few pedal rotations. If it drops, change down to a lower gear; if it increases, change into a higher gear.

Usually, you will need to adjust your gears only for hills. Change gears as soon as you lose forward momentum; it might be necessary to change several times in the course of an uphill run. When pedalling downhill, you should in general change to a higher gear before you start spinning the pedals. Downhill momentum will allow you to maintain your cadence part of the way up the next slope — usually for 5 to 15 metres.

When starting up a hill, be sure to change down before your cadence drops precipitously. For the derailleur to function, the chainwheel must spin evenly. If you change too late and exert too much pressure on the pedals, the derailleur may not respond. In that case, you will have to slow your cadence for a few pedal rotations to allow the gearing mechanism to click in properly. Good gearing requires anticipation.

In standard derailleur systems, moving the gear levers changes gears by skipping the chain from one cog and chainwheel to another. Bicycle derailleur/chainring systems vary, so you will have to become familiar with yours to know how far the gear levers must be moved to change gears. Allow several seconds for the derailleur to make the change. Index derailleur systems avoid some of the guesswork by clicking immediately into gear.

Braking

Effective braking is a vital bicycle-handling skill. However, proper braking technique is not only a safety factor, but also increases riding efficiency by allowing you to decelerate appropriately as required.

Most of the stopping force comes from the front brakes; while the rear brake does also exert some braking power, its main function is balance. Get into the habit of applying both brakes simultaneously, since operating just the front brake could lock the front wheel and send you tumbling over the bike. Moving your weight backwards on the saddle will also help you to stop more quickly.

Braking on wet or slippery roads requires special attention, because the brake pads slip on the rims. It may take three times as long to stop in wet conditions, and you are at a greater risk of skidding. Anticipate slow-downs, and apply the brakes gently, allowing yourself plenty of time to stop safely.

To slow or stop your bike gradually with your hands on the brake hoods, use the first two fingers of each hand to operate the levers *(right)*. If you are slowing, apply greater pressure to the front brake than the rear, and move your weight backwards slightly. To be prepared to make an abrupt halt, you should practise the emergency stopping technique *(inset)*. Apply both brakes, putting more pressure on the front brake. Simultaneously slide your weight all the way back behind the saddle to increase the pressure on the rear wheel. Your arms should be straight.

Riding in a Line

Riding in a straight line, and choosing a path round objects in the road as well as corners, sounds easier than it is. And following a line is an important skill that you must be able to maintain at all times. Not only does it make your movement predictable to cars and other riders, but it conserves the energy otherwise wasted in unnecessary side-to-side adjustments.

Ideally, you should follow a straight line about 15 centimetres from the shoulder of the road. Practise riding on a white line in an empty car park or a deserted stretch of road with no cars about. Then work on following the same line while you look over your shoulder.

Like most riding techniques, setting your line requires an awareness of the terrain and anticipation of what lies ahead. You want to veer from your line as little as possible: plan ahead for manoeuvres such as swerving round objects in your way or negotiating corners.

Riding in a line is a function of two elements: choosing the correct focal point and body position. Experts recommend focusing about 6 metres ahead of you when riding at 15 to 25 kilometres per hour; add about 15 centimetres for each additional kilometre per hour. This distance allows you to see obstacles ahead and to make subtle adjustments. Your wrists and elbows should be relaxed as you grip the handlebars *(above)*.

To avoid an obstacle in the road, use your hips to steer round it, leaning your body weight to the side as necessary. This will keep the front and rear tyres in alignment and conserve your energy *(left)*. Relying on your focal point will allow you to anticipate the correct line to follow round an obstacle on the basis of the road and traffic conditions *(below)*.

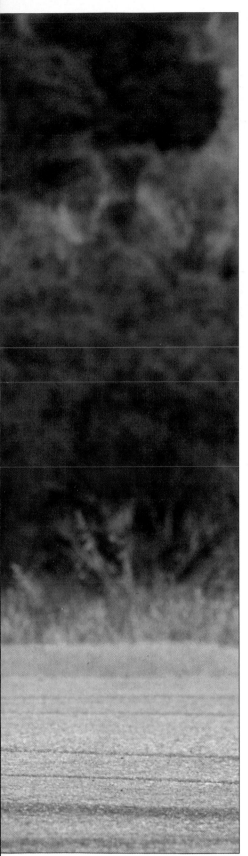

Cornering

Successful cornering is accomplished by shifts in body weight. You should never steer with the handlebars while you are actually in a turn; rather, you should position the bike to follow a wide arc that will also allow you to coast through it. Prior to encountering the turn, flick your brakes to slow down slightly, then lower your body and use a slight movement of your hips to lean in the direction of the turn *(left)*. Stop pedalling just before you enter the turn. Hold your pedals in the 12 o'clock/ six o'clock position, with your weight completely on the outside pedal and your leg extended, and your inside knee bent *(above)*. You should be able to lean more than 30 degrees in a turn and still stay balanced. Never brake abruptly while in a turn.

Hill Riding/1

Practise climbing short, gentle hills while seated *(above, left)*. Place your hands in the middle of the handlebars, and slide backwards slightly in the saddle to give yourself better leverage on the pedals. Use your arms to pull up slightly on the handlebars, rocking your upper body forwards rhythmically to increase your momentum. It is easier to climb steeper hills while standing on the pedals *(above, right)*. With your hands widely spaced on the brake hoods, shift your body weight over the front of the bike.

All of your bicycle-handling skills come into play when you tackle hills. Pedalling technique, gearing, braking, choosing a line and even cornering are included in a successful hill navigation. Hill climbing also demands a considerable amount of upper-body strength, as pulling on the handlebars allows you to increase the force that you apply on the pedals.

Gear selection should be based on staying as close as possible to your optimal cadence over level terrain. The gear to select depends on your fitness level, your climbing style and the gradient and length of the hill. In general, if you climb while standing on the pedals, you will ride in a higher gear than if you climb in a seated position. However, it is essential that you anticipate gear changes before you work too hard at the pedals on the uphill, which makes it difficult to change gears, or spin the pedals too quickly on the downhill stretch.

Avoid coasting after a long climb, even if you encounter a downhill immediately. It is better to keep your legs turning to avoid a build-up of lactic acid in your muscles.

Leveraging is an effective way to utilize your upper-body strength when climbing from a standing position *(left)*. With your hands in a wide grip on the brake hoods, shift your body weight forwards over the handlebars. As you perform each pedal downstroke, lean your body towards that leg to increase your pedalling force, alternating to left and right *(below)*. This will create the sensation that you are throwing your bike back and forth. Your front and rear tyres should stay in alignment as you climb.

Hill Riding/2

Maximizing both speed and safety is the goal of skilful descents. The primary danger in downhill riding is losing control on a curve. Prepare for curves by keeping your hands on the brake hoods, ready to use the brakes to reduce speed before you enter the curve *(right)*. Raising your upper body to increase wind resistance will also help slow the bike. Remember not to brake while actually cornering, and to steer the bike by leaning. The tucked position *(inset)* optimizes speed on a downhill straight: centre your body weight over the back of the saddle, keep your knees close together, place your hands next to the stem, and lower your body and head as close to the top tube as possible. To increase your balance, place your pedals in the three o'clock/ nine o'clock position.

Group Riding

Group riding, called riding the paceline, or draughting, is much more than social cycling. It is a time-honoured training technique that allows riders to benefit by protecting one another from the effects of wind resistance.

A paceline is a closely packed formation of riders, one behind the other. The lead rider is said to be pulling the rest, as they benefit from the draught created behind him or her, and studies have shown that paceline riding can save 20 to 25 per cent of a cyclist's energy. The paceline changes constantly, with a new rider assuming the lead position at a predetermined interval. Riding a paceline demands excellent bike-handling skills, since riders are only about 30 centimetres apart.

When riding a single paceline, all cyclists should follow about 30 centimetres behind the wheel of the preceding rider. The lead rider's pull lasts between one and 10 minutes. He then eases off to one side, and allows his speed to slow so he falls back to position 1. As the last rider passes him, he starts to accelerate and swings back into line behind him at position 2. The formation rotates continually, as the other riders maintain speed, and the second rider assumes his pull at the front.

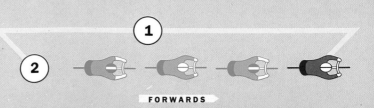

1

2

FORWARDS

An echelon is a paceline that is adjusted diagonally to minimize the effects of a crosswind. In an echelon, the riders are angled downwind from the leader, with the front wheel of each bicycle approximately aligned with the rear wheel of the preceding bike. The lead rider might pull for less than a minute. He then eases his pace, falling back to position 1 as he allows the second rider to pass him and assume the lead. After the last rider passes him, he accelerates and slips behind him into position 2.

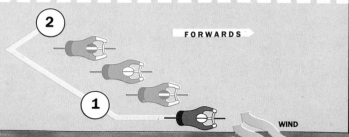

2

FORWARDS

1

WIND

All-Terrain Biking/1

The excitement and variety offered by all-terrain biking have made it the fastest-growing kind of cycling. Combining racing technology with the off-road capabilities of the popular children's BMX, or bicycle motocross, stunt bikes, these all-terrain bicycles — also called mountain bikes — can tackle steep, uneven trails. They have made accessible many areas formerly out of bounds to the rider and, because of the special handling skills required, have presented new challenges even to experienced cyclists. Indeed, the added element of rough terrain makes good bike-handling skills even more crucial to safe and efficient riding.

Even though ATBs are ideally suited for rugged terrain, one of the more popular uses of off-road bicycles is for urban riding. The knobby tyres that improve traction on uneven mountain trails do the same on pot-holed city roads. So, while its heavier frame means you will not be able to achieve the same on-road speeds with an ATB, it is perfectly appropriate as your only bicycle — unless you intend to get involved in road racing.

The off-road techniques on the following pages demonstrate specific handling skills for mountain bikes and show how they vary from those of traditional racing.

The upright posture is not as essential when riding your
ATB on a relatively smooth road, so bend your elbows to try
to lower yourself slightly into a more standard, aerodynamic
cycling position *(above)*.

A more upright posture and wider arm position *(left)* are the
primary variations between mountain and road bicycles. This
difference allows you to distribute your weight over a wider
area, thus increasing stability. When riding, focus on the path
ahead to prepare for any rocks, roots or gullies in your way.

Rising out of the saddle is usually the easiest way to go uphill on an ATB *(above)*. Bring your weight well forwards over the handlebars, keeping your arms widely spaced to balance the front wheel.

Controlling the bike is significantly more difficult as the terrain becomes more pitted and uneven *(above)*. Use your upper-body strength to control the front wheel, while maintaining your pedalling momentum for as long as possible. If pedalling slows so much as to become ineffective, walk your bike through the area to save energy *(right)*. Stabilize the bike by holding it at both the handlebar and the saddle.

All-Terrain Biking/3

Keep your weight as low as possible when riding downhill on an ATB to increase your stopping power. If you have a quick-release saddle, lower it just as you start down the hill. Shift your body backwards and plant your feet in the three o'clock/nine o'clock position *(right)*. Flick the brakes off and on, making sure not to hold the front brake too long, since it can lock the wheel. On steeper downhills *(inset)*, shift your weight to the rear of the saddle, with your arms outstretched, to stabilize the rear of the bike.

Strengtheners for Cyclists/1

Cycling is powered by the legs, particularly the quadriceps muscles in the front of the thigh. Strengthening exercises that work the hamstring muscles in the back of the thigh will help to balance this leg muscle development. This can make your cycling more effective, allowing you to push downwards and pull upwards on the pedals with equal force for proper pedalling action.

Strenuous uphill riding also makes substantial demands on the muscles of the upper body, so the strengthening programme on these two and the following four pages conditions the muscles of the shoulders and back, as well as those of the legs. Such exercises will enhance flexibility in these muscles, which often become stiff from long hours spent gripping the handlebars, while your torso is bent over on the saddle. A balanced strengthening programme that allows you to relax the muscles of your upper body will permit you to ride more comfortably for a longer time.

Stand straight with your arms at your sides. Bend your right knee and raise your leg to hip height, keeping your foot directly under your knee (above); lower and alternate legs; repeat 10 to 20 times.

Lie prone with your hands on the floor in a press-up position *(top)*. Perform a press-up, supporting your weight on your hands and feet *(above)*. Do not arch your back. Repeat 10 to 30 times.

Strengtheners for Cyclists/2

Stand straight with your arms at your sides, about 45 centimetres in front of a weight bench or low stool *(right)*. Simultaneously extend your arms in front of you and bend your knees. Keeping your lower back arched, continue lowering yourself into a squat. Stop just above the bench *(below)*; hold momentarily. Return to the starting position; repeat 10 to 20 times.

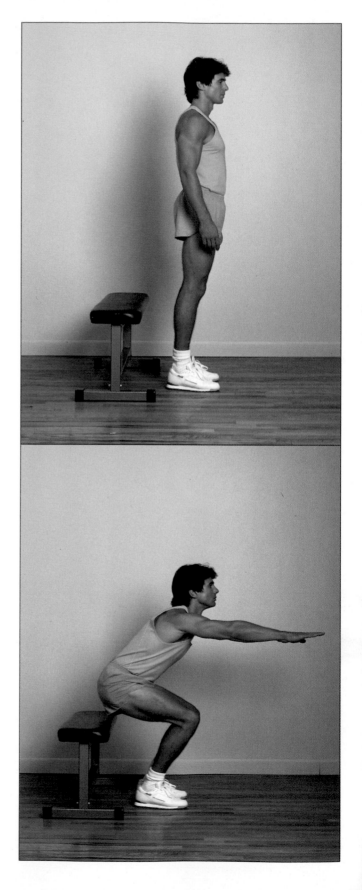

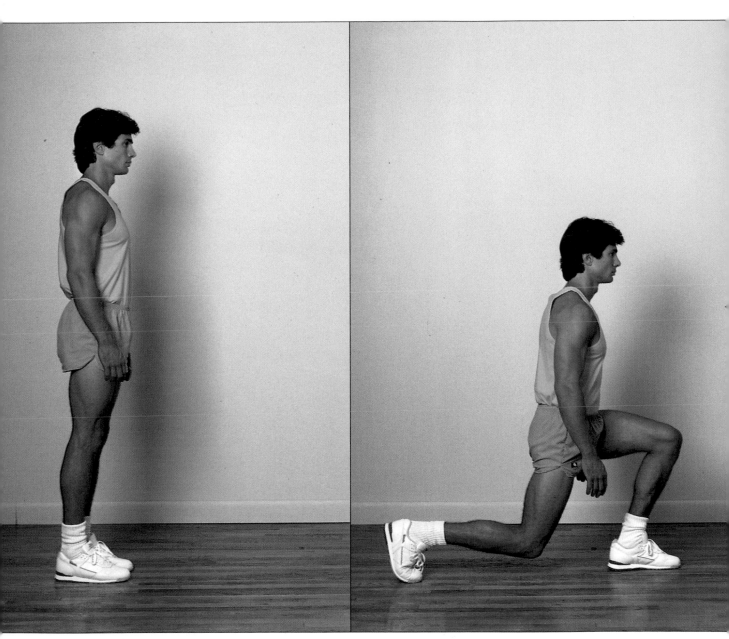

From a standing position *(above)*, lift your left leg up high and
lunge forwards as far as possible, dropping your right knee almost to
the ground *(above, right)*. Thrust backwards with your left leg and return
to the starting position; switch legs; repeat 10 to 20 times.

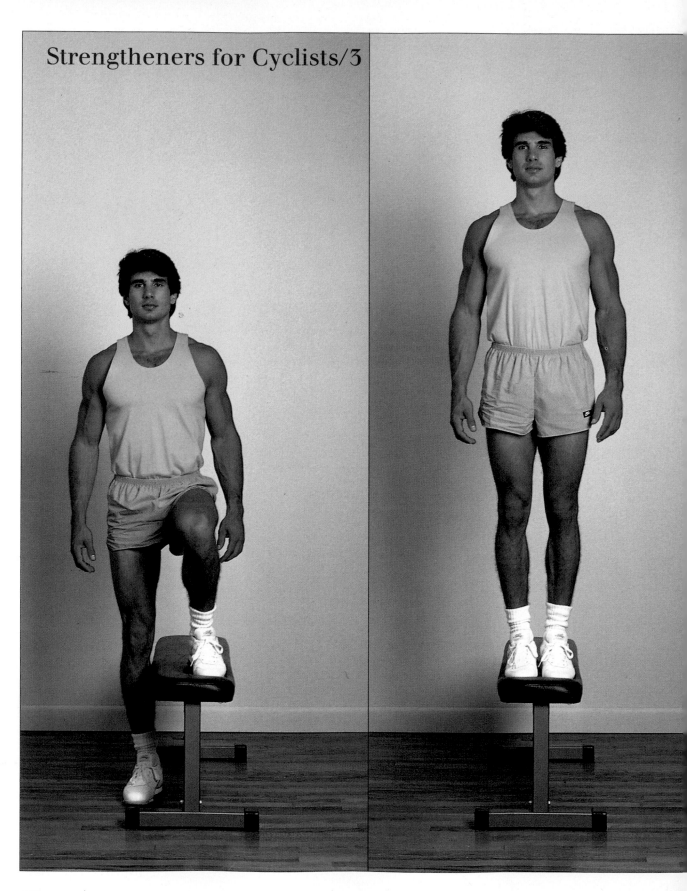

Stand next to a weight bench. Raise your left leg and rest your foot on the bench *(far left)*. Step up on to the bench with your right leg to a standing position *(centre)*, then lower your left leg back to the floor on the other side of the bench *(left)*. Alternate this stepping motion with both legs 10 to 20 times.

Stand with your back against a wall, your feet hip-width apart and about 50 centimetres away from it, and your arms crossed in front of your chest. Bend your knees and slide downwards so your thighs are parallel to the floor *(below)*. Hold for 20 to 60 seconds; return to the starting position; repeat two or three times.

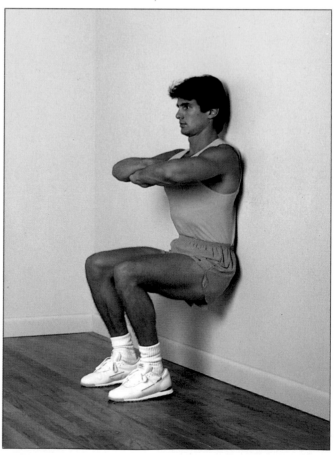

CHAPTER FOUR

The Triathlon

Using competition to improve the quality of your training

Because it combines three endurance activities, the competitive event known as the triathlon is virtually synonymous with cross training. Indeed, the increasing use of cross training by athletes and fitness enthusiasts exemplifies the growth of this varied, demanding sport, which most often combines swimming, cycling and running. In 1988, some 10,000 triathletes participated in about 150 triathlon events throughout the United Kingdom. In the most famous triathlon, the Ironman, competitors swim a gruelling 3.8 kilometres in open water, then cycle 180 kilometres and finish with a 42.2-kilometre marathon — a feat that the top contenders accomplish in less than nine hours.

However, you do not need to possess the almost superhuman level of endurance required for the Ironman to be a triathlete, since most triathlons are considerably less demanding. A more typical triathlon will consist of approximately a 1.5-kilometre swim, a 40-kilometre cycling leg and a 10-kilometre run. These distances, known collectively as the Short Course, are considered standard for each activity internationally.

And healthy individuals in reasonably good shape can train for a Short Course triathlon in about two months.

Successful triathletes attain their competitive goals by improving the quality of their workouts rather than increasing the quantity of them. A landmark study in the United States at Ball State University's human performance laboratory suggests that most triathletes would benefit from more interval training — short, intense workouts interspersed with rest periods — and fewer long swims, rides and runs. In the study, 11 triathletes were measured for body fat level and percentage of slow and fast-twitch muscle fibres, and for oxygen uptake in all three events. While most of the subjects were found to be strong and well trained aerobically, the major performance obstacle they faced was lack of technical skill. The researchers advised that once you have established a solid foundation of muscular and cardiovascular endurance in each sport, you should begin to incorporate speed work and increase your attention to technique.

The nine-week programme for a Short Course triathlon, on pages 108-113, maximizes the quality of your workouts. You are ready to undertake this programme if you have had at least three to six months of endurance, or distance, conditioning in each sport. At this point, you should begin a training regimen that includes both longer, anaerobic-threshold workouts and short, sprinting sets to increase your aerobic capacity and boost your fast-twitch fibre development for bursts of speed. You can tailor the programme to your individual needs by adding more sprint training or anaerobic threshold training for a specific event, by varying rest periods between intervals, or even by going back to an easier level if you feel you are overtraining.

Improving the quality of your workouts depends not only on developing your speed and endurance through interval training, but on enhancing your skill — your efficiency — in the three events. How much time you spend on technique should be based on your individual experience. For example, swimming usually consumes less time than the other two events in a triathlon, so swimming success is as dependent on technique as it is on endurance conditioning. Thus, your swimming programme will benefit most if you include drills, such as those in Chapter Two, that enhance stroke efficiency. Also, since most triathlon swims occur in open water, which requires coping with cold-water currents, try to practise in open water before you compete. Since one difficulty that open-water swimming presents is orientating yourself, it is a good idea to become familiar with marker buoys and landmarks of the actual course (see pages 116-117).

The cycling and running segments of a triathlon can be more demanding than the swimming event because the swim occurs first, when you are strongest, and both cycling and running require greater amounts of time to complete. The skills required for the cycling leg, such as ascending and descending hills while riding in a group, come from practice rides and from races. But draughting, the group-

Choosing a Race

The lengths, locations, dates and relative difficulty of triathlons vary greatly. Choosing which race to enter, and knowing when you are sufficiently trained to compete in such a race with confidence, can be quite difficult. Here are some guidelines:

◆ **Are you ready?** If you can swim 1 kilometre in 31 minutes or less, cycle 12 kilometres in no more than 34 minutes, and run 5 kilometres in no more than five minutes — all within a period of five days — you will be comfortable competing in the standard event of a 1.5-kilometre swim, a 40-kilometre cycle and a 10-kilometre run.

◆ **Which race should you enter?** Triathlons are staged in Britain from March to October. The lengths of races vary from the Mini-Triathlon, tailored especially for beginners, to the Ironman, consisting of a 3.8-kilometre open-water swim, a 180-kilometre cycle and a 42.2-kilometre marathon. Intermediate triathlons are the Short Course and the Long Course, which involves a 2-kilometre swim, a 90-kilometre cycle and a 20-kilometre run. Ideally, you should spend the night before the event near the course so that you will be well rested.

◆ **When should you enter?** Lists of forthcoming triathlons and biathlons (or two-sport competitions, usually of cycling and running) are available from the British Triathlon Association or from local triathlon clubs, and lists are also published in the *British Triathlon Handbook*.

riding technique demonstrated on pages 90-91 — a common energy-saving practice used in bike races — is not allowed in the triathlon.

Running is the final event of most triathlons, and many experts claim that it is the deciding factor since, if you are not at your absolute best during the swimming or cycling legs, you have a chance to make up lost time in the run. For this reason, the quality of your running workouts is of vital importance. It is not necessary to run an inordinate distance, especially since more injuries occur in training for this event than for any other. Rather, routines that allow you to boost your anaerobic threshold are invaluable.

The comprehensive muscle development of triathletes may lead to decreases in flexibility, requiring some special performance techniques in each sport. For example, since endurance runners tend to have less flexible ankles than competitive swimmers, a triathlete might benefit from using a shallow kick. Or, because runners tend to have less developed quadriceps than cyclists, a triathlete should utilize his or her hamstrings to get more pedalling power by positioning the saddle so that the downstroke leg is fully extended. The following pages will take you through the three sports of the triathlon and show you how to modify your technique to accommodate the muscle development caused by the endurance emphasis of cross training. They also demonstrate how to enhance your performance through drills, stretches and practising transitions.

Nine-Week Triathlon Training Programme

Optimizing your cross training regimen demands careful planning to ensure that you exercise all your muscles in a balanced way. Contrary to popular belief, this is not done by logging countless kilometres, which only increases the opportunity for injuries. Rather, elite triathletes emphasize the quality of workouts by including shorter, more intense sessions of anaerobic threshold and sprint training.

The nine-week training programme presented here was designed by premier triathlete Dave Scott, six-time winner of Hawaii's famed Ironman Triathlon. It will prepare you for an international-distance triathlon of a 1.5-kilometre swim, 40-kilometre bike ride and 10-kilometre run. Before embarking on the programme, you should have a basic level of aerobic fitness, with enough proficiency in each activity to be able to perform at least 20 consecutive minutes each of swimming, cycling and running.

You should work out six days each week on the programme, with two or three workout sessions on each day. Plan on investing about seven hours a week in your training to begin with; by the final week, you should have increased this amount to 12 hours a week. The workout times indicated include between three and eight minutes of warm-ups and between three and five minutes of cool-downs; use the longer warm-up time for the first event of the day, and the longer cool-down for the last segment.

Starting from Week 2, include a set of anaerobic threshold (AT) training in each event once a week. In Week 3, add a set of sprint training (ST) to each activity per week. The structuring of these shorter, more intense sessions is detailed on pages 110-113. Workouts not designated as AT or ST sessions should be performed as distance training at 60 to 85 per cent of your VO_2max time trial pace (*refer to the pace charts on pages 20-21*).

You can reorder your swim, cycle and run workouts and spread them throughout the day as your schedule permits. However, starting in Week 3, you should simulate a mini-triathlon on Saturdays: perform each event in triathlon sequence, complete with transitions. Allow yourself five-minute transitions to start with, and reduce this time as the weeks progress.

1

Su	M	Tu	W	Th	F	Sa
S-30	S-30	S-30		FREE	S-40	S-20
C-35	C-35	C-25	C-35	FREE		C-35
R-15	R-15		R-30	FREE	R-30	R-20

4

Su	M	Tu	W	Th	F	Sa
S-30 AT	S-35 ST	S-40 AT		FREE	S-40	S-30
C-40 AT	C-45	C-35	C-50 ST	FREE		C-50
R-25	R-20		R-35	FREE	R-35 ST	R-30

7

Su	M	Tu	W	Th	F	Sa
S-40 AT	S-45 ST	S-45	S-35	FREE	S-45	S-40
C-55 AT	C-60	C-40	C-70 ST	FREE	C-50 ST	C-60
R-35	R-30 ST		R-40 AT	FREE		R-45

2

Su	M	Tu	W	Th	F	Sa
S-30	S-30	S-30		FREE	S-40 AT	S-20
C-35 AT	C-35	C-25	C-35	FREE		C-35
R-15	R-15		R-30 AT	FREE	R-30	R-20

3

Su	M	Tu	W	Th	F	Sa
S-30 AT	S-35 ST	S-40 AT		FREE	S-40	S-30
C-40 AT	C-45	C-35	C-45 ST	FREE		C-45
R-25	R-20		R-35	FREE	R-35 ST	R-25

5

Su	M	Tu	W	Th	F	Sa
S-40 AT	S-40 ST	S-40	S-20	FREE	S-40	S-35
C-50 AT	C-55	C-35	C-60 ST	FREE		C-55
R-30	R-25		R-40 AT	FREE	R-45 ST	R-35

6

Su	M	Tu	W	Th	F	Sa
S-40 AT	S-40 ST	S-40	S-20	FREE	S-40	S-35
C-50 AT	C-55	C-35	C-65 ST	FREE		C-60
R-30	R-25		R-40 AT	FREE	R-45 ST	R-40

8

Su	M	Tu	W	Th	F	Sa
S-40 AT	S-45 ST	S-45	S-35	FREE	S-45	S-40
C-55 AT	C-60	C-40	C-70 ST	FREE	C-50 ST	C-70
R-35	R-30 ST		R-40 AT	FREE		R-50

9

Su	M	Tu	W	Th	F	Sa
S-30 AT	S-35 ST	S-40 AT		FREE	S-20	RACE DAY
C-40 AT	C-45	C-35	C-45 ST	FREE	C-20	RACE DAY
R-25	R-20 ST		R-35	FREE	R-15	RACE DAY

Anaerobic Threshold Training

For your anaerobic threshold training pace range, see page 21.

	SWIM	CYCLE	RUN
Interval duration	1.5-3 min.	1.5-3 min.	1.5-3 min.
Interval distance	45-275 m	0.6-2.4 km	275-730 m
Number of repeats	8-30	8-30	8-30
Rest interval	10-45 sec.	15 sec.-1 min.	15 sec.-1 min.
Training frequency	Once or twice per week	Once or twice per week	Once or twice per week
Sample workouts for each event	20 x 50 m	8 x 1.2 km	8 x 400 m
	4 x 250 m 3 x 200 m 2 x 100 m	3 x 0.5 km 1 x 1.5 km 3 x 0.5 km 1 x 1.5 km 3 x 0.5 km 1 x 1.5 km	1 x 200 m 1 x 300 m 1 x 400 m 2 x 500 m 1 x 400 m 1 x 300 m 1 x 200 m

Anaerobic Threshold Training

Your anaerobic threshold is the point at which lactic acid is being synthesized faster than your muscles can diffuse it into your bloodstream. This causes you to feel intense fatigue, so you will only be able to sustain exercise at a level beyond your anaerobic threshold for a short time. Through training, you can boost this threshold so that you are able to push yourself further and faster without crossing it. This is done through interval work that trains your fast-twitch fibres to function more efficiently, thus delaying the build-up of lactic acid.

Perform a series of short intervals of 1.5 to three minutes at 75 to 90 per cent of your VO_2max. Check the pace charts on pages 20-21 to determine your appropriate pace range based on your time trial. How long to rest between intervals varies from person to person; the time you will need is determined by your genetically determined distribution of fast and slow-twitch fibres. If you have more fast-twitch fibres, you will require less rest between intervals than if your slow-twitch fibres predominate. Thus, determine the rest period between intervals by how you feel. In general, you should allow your heart rate to drop only 10 to 15 per cent between repeats. But if you find your muscles burn and feel heavy, you should probably increase the rest interval.

Use the guidelines on the left to structure your AT sessions in a variety of ways, as the sample workout sets illustrate. However, the actual intervals in each AT session should total at least 15 minutes.

Sprint Training

Sprinting will improve your performance times, since it enables you to function with oxygen debt and to endure lactic acid build-up. Sprint training requires that you perform very short intervals at all-out, 100-per cent effort and at speeds that exceed your VO_2max time trial pace.

You can sustain these speeds because the intervals performed are so brief — from 10 seconds to two minutes and covering minimum distances. But because they entail such an intense effort, your rest time between the sprints should be three times the length of the actual sprint *(see the chart on the right)*. During the rest period, keep moving at a very slow speed. This is called active rest; it helps minimize lactic acid build-up.

Use the pace chart for sprint training on pages 20-21 to determine your appropriate interval training pace, based on your time trial. Then use the guidelines on the right to design your own sprint training workouts for each activity. Start at a low number of repeats — four per workout — and increase the amount as your body adapts to this training. You can measure the interval lengths by either distance or time, as shown in the sample workouts. Vary the composition of your intervals. For example, you may repeat the same distance, such as four 100-metre intervals, making sure that you rest between each one for three times as long as it takes to perform; or you may decrease the distances covered in your workouts periodically, and ladder your intervals, which involves increasing the distances and then decreasing them again.

Sprint Training
For your sprint training pace range, see page 21.

	SWIM	CYCLE	RUN
Interval duration	10 sec.-2 min.	10 sec.-2 min.	10 sec.-2 min.
Interval distance	15-115 m	100-1,600 m	75-400 m
Number of repeats	4-8	4-8	4-8
Work/rest ratio	1:3	1:3	1:3
Training frequency	Once or twice per week	Once or twice per week	Once per week
Sample workouts for each event	4 x 100 m	4 x 800 m	6 x 75 m
	3 x 75 m 2 x 50 m 1 x 25 m	2 x 400 m 1 x 800 m 2 x 400 m 2 x 200 m	2 x 400 m 2 x 300 m 2 x 100 m

To compensate for tight shoulders, perform a slower, more powerful catch, with your wrist flexed and bent outwards about 20 to 30 degrees *(above)*.

Maximize propulsion at the finish by hyperextending your wrist so that your palm faces directly backwards *(below)*.

If you have tight arms and shoulders, a wide recovery, with your hand higher than your elbow, will help to relax your shoulders *(above)*.

Swimming

While swimming is almost always the first event in a triathlon, it is usually the shortest leg of the race. Because it comprises a smaller percentage of your total triathlon effort, most triathletes do not choose to perform an all-out swim.

The physiology of swimming makes it aerobically less demanding than either of the other two sports: being horizontal in the water allows your cardiovascular system to pump as much as 20 per cent more blood to your muscles than when you are in a vertical position. To maximize your training, work on improving stroke mechanics, using the techniques shown in Chapter Two as a guide, and conserve leg strength.

The muscle development that results from cross training can change stroke mechanics slightly, requiring some adjustments to maintain good form. For example, because they keep their arms forwards while cycling, triathletes generally have less flexibility in their shoulders than do other swimmers, resulting in a wider catch and higher arm recovery. Methods for dealing with such differences are shown on these two pages; preparing to swim in open water appears on pages 116-117.

Kicking should contribute only a little to your forward propulsion; save energy by keeping your kick shallow. Turning your toes inwards slightly will increase your kicking efficiency and power *(below)*.

Practise sighting when swimming in a pool. Pick a landmark in front of you at the pool's edge, and raise your head straight out of the water to look forwards at it every five strokes *(above)*.

Open-Water Swimming

For many triathletes, swimming in an ocean or a lake presents the greatest challenge of the race. Open-water swimming is vastly different from pool swimming: the water is generally colder and there may be waves or currents; there are no lane markers for guidance. In addition, you may have to contend with the flailing arms and legs of the other competitors.

Training for triathlon swimming requires some open-water sessions to get you acclimatized to the colder temperature and familiar with lane-less navigation. Start with short, 15-minute workouts, and increase the time gradually. Be sure to wear a swimming cap, which will greatly reduce heat loss.

At the start of the race, manoeuvre through surf by diving beneath waves just before they break over you. Try not to be intimidated by the congestion at the start; at worst, you will sustain a kick, but it will be cushioned by the water. As the crowd thins, take advantage of other swimmers' forward propulsion by draughting, which is allowed in this event and can save up to 20 per cent of your energy: follow slightly behind a swimmer going as fast or a little faster than you.

Sighting — keeping track of landmarks and buoys — keeps you on course as you navigate through open water. This can be especially difficult when you are moving fast. A sighting drill is shown above.

Occasional bilateral breathing — breathing to both sides —
will help keep you on course when swimming in open water,
and will also alleviate shoulder discomfort.

Cycling

A majority of triathletes say that cycling is their weakest area. As in the other events, to accommodate the comprehensive muscle development of cross trainers as well as to conserve leg strength for running, you might need to make some specific adjustments in your cycling technique.

In particular, triathletes have well-developed hamstrings from running. To take full advantage of this, you should emphasize your downstroke pedalling, rather than striving for the more balanced pedalling that other cyclists favour, which relies mainly on the quadriceps for the upstroke. You should also work at a cadence of about 80 to 95 rpms, which places more emphasis on your slow-twitch endurance fibres. On hills, reduce your cadence even further, to 60 rpms, or experiment with standing and using a higher gear.

To build up your quadriceps for cycling — and enhance your anaerobic training — change into high gear and pedal while standing. Perform four to eight repetitions for 20 to 60 seconds.

Aerodynamic handlebars *(left)* streamline your body posture, and have been shown to shave over a minute off every 40 kilometres. Varying your hand position on the handlebars frequently relaxes your triceps, deltoids and lower back; similarly, standing on the pedals stretches your lower back *(inset, far left)*. To accommodate differing patterns of muscle development, optimal sizing of your bike for a triathlon is slightly different from sizing for regular cycling. The saddle should be raised higher so your leg can be fully extended *(inset, left)* to allow for a more powerful downstroke.

Running

Triathletes tend to be strong runners. However, running is the last leg of the race, so your technique will be hampered by muscles that have tightened in the swimming and cycling events. On the other hand, strengthening your upper body through swimming will allow you to use your upper body muscles to help power you through the early part of the run.

When changing from cycling to running, you also have to contend with tight shoulder and back muscles from the bent-over cycling posture, and tight hip flexors from the continual hip rotation of pedalling. Concentrate on your respiration, taking slow, deep breaths, to help ease you into the run. Start with a shortened stride to accommodate tight hip flexors and allow your hamstrings to adjust to the workload. Increase your stride gradually as your muscles become more flexible. Do not lift your legs too high, since this places more stress on your hamstrings and hip flexors, also causing you to land harder, which increases the pounding absorbed by your feet and knees. Instead, increase the rate of your stride, rather than your stride length, for the first kilometre or so, then return to your earlier rate.

To align your body correctly for triathlon running, shift your weight by leaning your upper body forwards about five degrees *(above)*. Lower your head slightly; focus your eyes **12 to 15** metres ahead.

Keeping your upper body, including your face, relaxed will help
you run more smoothly. Every kilometre or so, drop your shoulders
and shake your arms and fingers to facilitate relaxation *(above)*.

Transitions

Experienced triathletes know the value of smooth transitions: the amount of time you spend changing from one leg of a triathlon to the next can decide the race. Becoming proficient at transitions requires practice, so include them in your training programme.

Effective transitions actually begin before the race, at your assigned transition location. Here, well in advance of the starting gun, you should organize the clothing and gear required for the race. Plan this layout so that the changes you will need to make during the race are minimal. For example, wear your swimsuit for the entire race, if possible. Many triathletes do not wear socks, to save the time it takes to put them on.

Transitions include the actual physiological preparations you make for changing activities as well. Thus, use the moments immediately preceding and following transitions for warm-up and cool-down stretches.

Have your transition gear laid out in a well-planned fashion *(above)*. Arrange your gear according to use: in front, have a towel for drying your feet. Behind this, place your shoes — ready to be tied (and socks, if you wear them) — and a rolled-up singlet. Your bike should be at the back. Position your helmet on the handlebars or at the front wheel, with your gloves and sunglasses inside it.

If you have a clip-on pedal/shoe system, you can save time in the swim-to-bike transition by putting your shoes on while you begin riding *(right)*. Rub the inside rim of the shoes with petroleum jelly to make them slip on more easily.

Anticipate transitions by doing some preliminary stretches in the moments before you finish an event. In the final stages of the cycling segment, stretch your back and hip flexors by placing your hands on the brake hoods and lowering yourself off the saddle, pushing your hips towards the stem. Drop one heel all the way downwards, hold momentarily, then switch heel positions. Look up slightly and arch your back *(below)*.

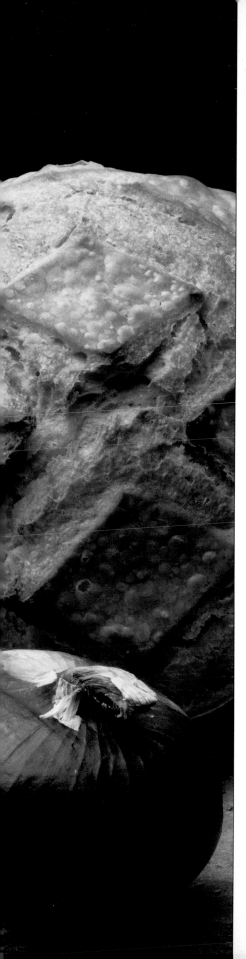

CHAPTER FIVE

Eating for Performance

The facts about carbohydrate loading

If you are serious about your endurance training, what should you eat to maximize your performance? Almost twenty years ago, a team of Swedish researchers rigorously addressed this question by developing a dietary programme to help endurance athletes increase their exercise time before becoming exhausted. The key to their programme lay in manipulating an athlete's intake of carbohydrates, nutrients that are very important for fuelling muscular endurance. The human body converts carbohydrates in food into blood sugar and glycogen, a form of carbohydrate that is stored in the muscles and the liver. When the supply of muscle glycogen is depleted, muscle fibres are no longer able to contract efficiently and fatigue occurs. Therefore, a diet that could either postpone glycogen depletion or increase the muscles' ability to store glycogen would be a boon to endurance athletes.

Carbohydrate loading, as the Swedish regimen came to be known, involved a two-step process: depletion and loading. One week before a competitive event, the athlete would first deplete his glycogen stores

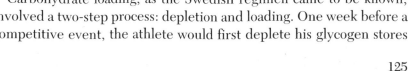

by exercising to exhaustion for three days while consuming a low-carbohydrate diet. Three or four days before competition, the athlete would reduce his exercise workload significantly and switch to a high-carbohydrate diet; the glycogen-starved muscles would then compensate for their depleted state by absorbing glycogen to the point of supersaturation. In studies conducted by the Swedish researchers, subjects stored two to three times the normal amount of muscle glycogen and increased the length of time they could exercise.

Many athletes have found, however, that this classic method of carbohydrate loading is not always the most beneficial: not only does the regimen disrupt normal training and diet patterns, but the forced depletion of carbohydrates does not appear to enhance a trained muscle's ability to replenish glycogen. Well-trained athletes naturally deplete muscle glycogen during the course of their day-to-day exercise programmes. As an adaptation to training, muscle fibres increase their capacity for storing glycogen if adequate carbohydrates are in the diet. Moreover, sharply depleting the body's glycogen level has caused physiological side effects such as dizziness, soreness and fatigue; the subsequent loading phase may in turn be accompanied by water retention so that an athlete feels bloated and stiff. For these reasons, a growing number of nutritionists and sports medicine specialists have advised that the depletion and deprivation phases of carbohydrate loading should be avoided.

Most experts, in fact, now recommend that you forego any phase of a diet that emphasizes low levels of carbohydrates. You can prepare yourself for even the heaviest training programmes by eating what is now considered to be a well-balanced diet. As the guidelines on the opposite page indicate, you should obtain about 55 to 60 per cent of your calories from carbohydrates, preferably complex ones such as vegetables, pulses, breads, cereals and pastas.

To prepare for a competition, you can commence an extra-high carbohydrate diet three or four days prior to the actual event. This diet should contain your usual number of calories, but increase the percentage of carbohydrate calories to 70 to 80 per cent. Use the recipes in this chapter, almost all of which are in that range, to help plan your meals. Be sure to consume plenty of fluids during this carbohydrate-loading phase, as well as during the competition itself.

Eat your last big high-carbohydrate meal 14 to 16 hours before your event. Avoid very spicy, salty or high-fibre foods, which can upset your digestive system. At bedtime the night before you compete, have a high-carbohydrate snack, such as the Apple-Sultana Scones on page 129 or the Dosas on page 141. Then have an additional snack three to fours hours prior to competition.

This modified regimen has been shown to work effectively. In several studies, athletes who followed a diet deriving 70 per cent of its calories from carbohydrates did not suffer from a low level of glycogen even after several successive days of prolonged, vigorous

The Basic Guidelines

For a moderately active adult, Britain's National Advisory Committee on Nutrition Education recommends a diet that is low in fat, high in carbohydrates and moderate in protein. The committee's proposals for the long term suggest that no more than 30 per cent of your calories come from fat, that around 11 per cent come from protein and hence that 55 to 60 per cent come from carbohydrates. A gram of fat equals nine calories, while a gram of protein or carbohydrate equals four calories; therefore, if you eat 2,100 calories a day, you should consume approximately 70 grams of fat, 310 grams of carbohydrate and 60 grams of protein daily. If you follow a low-fat/high-carbohydrate diet, your chance of developing heart disease, cancer and other life-threatening diseases may be considerably reduced.

◆ The nutrition charts that accompany each of the low-fat/high-carbohydrate recipes in this book include the number of calories per serving, the number of grams of fat, carbohydrate and protein in a serving, and the percentage of calories derived from each of these nutrients. In addition, the charts provide the amount of calcium, iron and sodium per serving.

◆ Calcium deficiency may be associated with periodontal diseases — which attack the mouth's bones and tissues, including the gums — in both men and women, and with osteoporosis, or bone shrinking and weakening, in elderly women. The deficiency may also contribute to high blood pressure. The daily allowance for calcium recommended by the United Kingdom Department of Health and Social Security (DHSS) is 500 milligrams a day for men and women. Pregnant and lactating women are advised to consume 1,200 milligrams daily.

◆ Although one way you can reduce your fat intake is to cut your consumption of red meat, you should make sure that you get your necessary iron from other sources. The DHSS suggests a minimum of 10 milligrams of iron per day for men and 12 milligrams for women between the ages of 18 and 54.

◆ High sodium intake is associated with high blood pressure in susceptible people. Most adults should restrict sodium intake to about 2,000 milligrams a day, according to the World Health Organization. One way to keep sodium consumption in check is not to add table salt to food.

exercise. In comparison, subjects who followed a diet in which only 40 to 50 per cent of the calories came from carbohydrates had less available glycogen. Researchers have also found that loading up on carbohydrates following an endurance event is an effective way to rebuild glycogen reserves. One university study showed that athletes who consumed carbohydrates within two hours after a strenuous exercise session stored more carbohydrates from the meal than subjects who waited for a longer period.

Bear in mind, however, that carbohydrate loading will only benefit you for non-stop events or intense training sessions that last longer than 90 minutes. For middle-distance races, extra carbohydrates do not appear to offer any advantage. More important, carbohydrate loading cannot compensate for the lack of a sound diet or training; only well-trained muscles can put extra carbohydrates to use.

Five-Vegetable Fry-Up

Breakfast

FIVE-VEGETABLE FRY-UP

CALORIES per serving	250
73% Carbohydrate	47 g
7% Protein	5 g
20% Fat	6 g
CALCIUM	68 mg
IRON	2 mg
SODIUM	209 mg

Carbohydrates fuel your body, but vitamins are also vital for optimal health. This dish supplies more than 50 milligrams of vitamin C.

500 g (1 lb) new potatoes	60 g (2 oz) shallots
250 g (8 oz) carrots	2 teaspoons margarine
250 g (8 oz) parsnips	1 tablespoon olive oil
125 g (4 oz) orange-fleshed sweet potatoes	2 teaspoons sugar
	¼ teaspoon salt
125 g (4 oz) turnips	½ teaspoon black pepper
1 onion	4 tablespoons chopped parsley

Wash and trim the new potatoes, carrots, parsnips, sweet potatoes and turnips, and cut them into 1 cm (½ inch) thick slices. Bring 17.5 cl (6 fl oz) of water to the boil in a large non-stick frying pan over medium-high heat. Add the vegetables, bring the water back to the boil and cover the pan. Cook for 5 to 7 minutes, until the vegetables are tender but still crisp, stirring several times. Meanwhile, peel and thinly slice the onion and shallots.

Transfer the cooked vegetables to a bowl and cover it loosely with foil. Wipe the frying pan with paper towels. Melt the margarine in the pan over medium heat, then add the onion and shallots, and sauté for 2 minutes, or until the onion is golden. Discard any liquid from the bowl and return the vegetables to the pan, then add the oil, sugar and salt. Cook, stirring frequently from the bottom of the pan, for 10 to 15 minutes, until the vegetables are tender and browned. Add the pepper to taste and sprinkle over the parsley. Divide among four plates, and serve at once.   Makes 4 servings

WHOLEMEAL QUICK BREAD

A thick slice of bread is a good foundation for breakfast. Top it with a fruit spread or low-fat ricotta or mozzarella cheese.

75 g (2½ oz) plain flour
175 g (6 oz) wholemeal flour
1 teaspoon baking powder
¾ teaspoon bicarbonate of soda
Pinch of salt

25 cl (8 fl oz) buttermilk
100 g (3½ oz) honey
**15 g (½ oz) margarine, melted
    and cooled**
1 egg, lightly beaten

CALORIES per serving	180
74% Carbohydrate	35 g
12% Protein	6 g
14% Fat	3 g
CALCIUM	77 mg
IRON	1 mg
SODIUM	206 mg

Preheat the oven to 180°C (350°F or Mark 4). Lightly oil a 20 cm (8 inch) round baking tin and dust it with a little plain flour. In a medium-sized bowl, stir together the flours, baking powder, bicarbonate of soda and salt, and make a well in the centre. Add the buttermilk, honey and margarine to the egg, then add the egg mixture to the dry ingredients and stir until just combined. Turn the batter into the tin and bake for 35 minutes, or until a toothpick inserted in the centre of the bread comes out clean and dry. Turn the bread out on to a rack to cool before serving.   Makes 8 servings

APPLE-SULTANA SCONES

A pre-workout breakfast of fruit-filled scones offers plenty of carbohydrates to ensure a ready supply of energy for exercise.

300 g (10 oz) plain flour
2 tablespoons brown sugar
2 teaspoons baking powder
½ teaspoon ground cinnamon
Pinch of salt

**45 g (1½ oz) margarine, well
    chilled**
17.5 cl (6 fl oz) skimmed milk
**60 g (2 oz) dried apples, coarsely
    chopped**
45 g (1½ oz) sultanas

CALORIES per scone	85
73% Carbohydrate	16 g
8% Protein	2 g
19% Fat	2 g
CALCIUM	39 mg
IRON	1 mg
SODIUM	79 mg

Preheat the oven to 220°C (425°F or Mark 7). In a medium-sized bowl, stir together the flour, sugar, baking powder, cinnamon and salt. Using your fingertips, rub in the margarine until the mixture resembles coarse crumbs. Stir in the milk, then add the apples and sultanas, and stir until just combined. Form the dough into a ball on a lightly floured work surface and, using a lightly floured rolling pin, roll it out to a 22 cm (9 inch) circle about 1 cm (½ inch) thick. Using a 5 cm (2 inch) biscuit cutter, cut 20 scones. Place them on a non-stick baking sheet and bake for 10 minutes, or until golden-brown.

                                                              Makes 20 scones

Lunch

OAT BREAD

Oats are a whole grain: they retain their bran layer. Oat bran is particularly beneficial as it is rich in soluble fibre, which has been shown to reduce blood cholesterol. Aerobic exercise may also help lower cholesterol levels.

CALORIES per serving	165
78% Carbohydrate	32 g
15% Protein	6 g
7% Fat	1 g
CALCIUM	35 mg
IRON	2 mg
SODIUM	22 mg

250 g (8 oz) wholemeal flour
375 g (13 oz) plain flour
100 g (3½ oz) rolled oats
7 g (¼ oz) easy-blend dried yeast

Pinch of salt
25 cl (8 fl oz) skimmed milk
2 tablespoons brown sugar
1 egg

In a medium-sized bowl, stir together the wholemeal flour, 250 g (8 oz) of plain flour, 90 g (3 oz) of rolled oats, the yeast and salt, and make a well in the centre; set aside.

Combine the milk, sugar and 25 cl (8 fl oz) of water in a small saucepan over low heat and bring it to 43°C (110°F) — just warm to the touch. Meanwhile, separate the egg; place the white in a small bowl, cover with plastic film and set aside. Beat the yolk in a small bowl, then beat in 4 tablespoons of the milk mixture. Add both milk mixtures to the dry ingredients, and stir until a dough forms. Turn the dough on to a lightly floured surface and knead it for 5 to 7 minutes, kneading in the remaining plain flour as needed. Place the

Oat Bread

dough in a medium-sized bowl, cover it with a damp tea towel and set aside in a warm place to rise for 45 minutes, or until doubled in bulk.

Preheat the oven to 200°C (400°F or Mark 6). Lightly oil a baking sheet. Knock back the dough and knead it on a lightly floured surface for 1 to 2 minutes. Form the dough into a 20 cm (8 inch) round and place it on the baking sheet; set aside, uncovered, for 15 minutes. Beat the egg white and spread it generously over the top of the loaf with a pastry brush, then sprinkle the loaf with the remaining oats. Bake for 25 minutes, or until the bread is golden-brown and sounds hollow when tapped on the bottom. Cool the bread on a rack before serving.   Makes 16 servings

CHUNKY FRUIT BUTTER

This sandwich filling is low in fat and therefore far more healthy than a mayonnaise-dressed salad. Natural sugars in the fruit provide abundant carbohydrates.

2 large Granny Smith apples	**45 g (1½ oz) raisins**
125 g (4 oz) dried apricots	**¼ teaspoon ground ginger**

Core but do not peel the apples; cut them into large chunks. Bring 2.5 cm (2 inches) of water to the boil in a pan that will hold a steamer. Place all the fruit in the steamer, cover the pan and reduce the heat so that the water simmers. Steam for 10 to 15 minutes, until the apples are tender when pierced with the tip of a knife. Transfer the fruit to a food processor or blender, add the ginger and process for 1 minute, or until blended but still chunky. (If you prefer a smoother butter, process the fruit until puréed.) Transfer to a jar, cover and refrigerate. The fruit butter will keep for up to a week.

Makes 10 servings (about 2 tablespoons each)

CALORIES per serving	60
94% Carbohydrate	16 g
4% Protein	1 g
2% Fat	0.2 g
CALCIUM	10 mg
IRON	1 mg
SODIUM	2 mg

VEGETABLE PURÉE SANDWICH

This sandwich is an outstanding source of vitamins A and C, and also contains a substantial amount of iron. Iron deficiency can hinder aerobic endurance by decreasing oxygen transport in the body's tissues.

250 g (8 oz) carrots	**2 tablespoons chopped fresh dill**
250 g (8 oz) turnips	**1 small cucumber**
250 g (8 oz) orange-fleshed sweet	**Eight 1 cm (½ inch) thick slices**
** potatoes**	** Vegetable Bread (page 133)**
1 tablespoon Dijon mustard	

Trim the carrots, and peel the turnips and sweet potatoes; cut them into large chunks. Bring 2.5 cm (1 inch) of water to the boil in a pan that will hold a large steamer. Place the vegetables in the steamer and cook, covered, for 10 minutes, or until tender when pierced with a sharp knife; set aside to cool.

Place the vegetables in a medium-sized bowl and mash them until smooth. Add the mustard and dill, and stir until blended; set aside. Peel and slice the cucumber. Toast the bread and spread about one quarter of the vegetable purée on each of four slices. Top with the cucumber slices and a second slice of toast. Serve immediately.   Makes 4 servings

CALORIES per serving	405
77% Carbohydrate	80 g
12% Protein	12 g
11% Fat	5 g
CALCIUM	93 mg
IRON	4 mg
SODIUM	597 mg

CALORIES per serving	115
70% Carbohydrate	20 g
10% Protein	3 g
20% Fat	3 g
CALCIUM	14 mg
IRON	1 mg
SODIUM	96 mg

RYE BREAD

You should eat a high-carbohydrate meal within two hours after exercising in order to replenish your body's glycogen stores most efficiently. Fulfil your need for carbohydrates by planning this meal around a home-made bread such as this one. The yeast in the bread adds biotin, a B vitamin that plays a role in glycogen synthesis.

150 g (5 oz) light rye flour
125 g (4 oz) wholemeal flour
150 g (5 oz) plain flour
½ teaspoon salt
7 g (¼ oz) dried yeast
2 tablespoons molasses

1 tablespoon cider vinegar
2 tablespoons malted grain
  beverage mix (instant
  coffee substitute)
45 g (1½ oz) margarine, melted
2 teaspoons caraway seeds

In a medium-sized bowl, stir together all the flours and the salt, and make a well in the centre; set aside. Place the yeast in a small bowl, add 4 tablespoons of warm water (40-45°C/105-115° F) and set aside for 2 to 3 minutes. Meanwhile, in a small bowl stir together the molasses, vinegar, grain beverage mix and 17.5 cl (6 fl oz) of water. Pour the yeast mixture, the molasses mixture, the margarine and caraway seeds into the dry ingredients, and stir to form a dough. Turn the dough on to a lightly floured surface and knead it for 5 to 7 minutes, until smooth and elastic. Transfer the dough to a medium-sized bowl, cover it with a damp tea towel and set aside in a warm place to rise for 1 hour, or until doubled in bulk.

Knock back the dough and knead it for 2 minutes on a lightly floured surface. Return the dough to the bowl, cover and let it rise for about 30 minutes, or until almost doubled in bulk.

Lightly oil a 22 by 12 cm (9 by 5 inch) loaf tin and dust it lightly with flour. Knock back the dough again and roll it into a ball with your hands, then flatten it into a 20 cm (8 inch) disc. Roll up the dough to form a log. Place the dough in the tin and set it aside to rise, uncovered, for 30 minutes.

Preheat the oven to 230°C (450°F or Mark 8). Bake the bread for 10 minutes, then reduce the oven temperature to 170°C (325°F or Mark 3) and bake for 35 minutes more, or until it is golden-brown and sounds hollow when tapped. Turn out on a rack to cool for at least 10 minutes before serving.

Makes 16 servings

CALORIES per serving	115
73% Carbohydrate	22 g
17% Protein	5 g
10% Fat	1 g
CALCIUM	34 mg
IRON	2 mg
SODIUM	34 mg

CREAMY MUSHROOM BARLEY SOUP

This soup is a good source of niacin, a B vitamin that plays a part in the body's release of energy from carbohydrates.

250 g (8 oz) onions
2 garlic cloves
50 cl (16 fl oz) low-sodium
  chicken stock

6 tablespoons pearl barley
250 g (8 oz) mushrooms
4 tablespoons chopped parsley
2 tablespoons chopped fresh dill

Peel and coarsely chop the onions and garlic; set aside. Bring the stock and 50 cl (16 fl oz) of water to the boil in a medium-sized saucepan over medium-high heat. Stir in the onions, garlic and barley, cover the pan, reduce the heat to low and simmer for 45 minutes. Meanwhile, wipe, trim and coarsely chop the mushrooms; set aside.

Add the mushrooms to the soup, cover the pan and simmer for another 15 minutes. Using a slotted spoon, transfer the solids to a food processor or blender and process until puréed. Return the purée to the saucepan, and stir in the parsley and dill. Bring the soup to the boil over medium-high heat, then ladle it into four bowls and serve.   Makes 4 servings

VEGETABLE BREAD

Carrots are an excellent source of beta carotene, which the body converts into vitamin A. Research has revealed vitamin A to be involved in glycogen synthesis and in the synthesis of muscle protein, two functions important in endurance and strength training.

CALORIES per serving	155
75% Carbohydrate	29 g
13% Protein	5 g
12% Fat	2 g
CALCIUM	23 mg
IRON	2 mg
SODIUM	161 mg

200 g (7 oz) cooked red kidney beans, or canned red kidney beans, rinsed and drained
250 g (8 oz) carrots, grated
250 g (8 oz) spring onions, finely chopped
2 garlic cloves, crushed

7 g (¼ oz) dried yeast
450 g (15 oz) plain flour
150 g (5 oz) wholemeal flour
1 teaspoon salt
½ teaspoon ground pepper
30 g (1 oz) margarine

Mash the beans in a medium-sized bowl, then add the carrots, spring onions and garlic, and stir until combined; set aside. Place the yeast in a small bowl, add 17.5 cl (6 fl oz) of warm water (40-45°C/105-115°F) and set aside for 2 to 3 minutes. Meanwhile, in a large bowl stir together the plain flour, 125 g (4 oz) of wholemeal flour, the salt and pepper, and make a well in the centre. Pour in the yeast mixture, the vegetables and the margarine, and stir until well combined; the mixture will form a fairly sticky dough. Flour the work surface with 2 tablespoons of wholemeal flour. Knead the dough for 5 to 7 minutes, until smooth and elastic, kneading in more flour if necessary. Transfer the dough to a medium-sized bowl, cover it with a damp tea towel and set aside in a warm place to rise for 1 to 1½ hours, until doubled in bulk.

Knock back the dough. Sprinkle another 2 tablespoons of wholemeal flour on the work surface and knead the dough for 2 minutes. Return the dough to the bowl, cover and let it rise for about 1 hour, or until almost doubled in bulk.

Lightly oil a baking sheet. Knock back the dough again and knead it briefly on a lightly floured surface. Form the dough into an 18 cm (7 inch) round and place it on a baking sheet to rise, uncovered, for 30 minutes.

Preheat the oven to 220°C (425°F or Mark 7). Bake the bread for 10 minutes, then reduce the oven temperature to 170°F (325°F or Mark 3) and bake for 45 to 50 minutes more, until the loaf is golden-brown and sounds hollow when tapped. Turn the bread out on to a rack to cool for at least 10 minutes before serving.   Makes 16 servings

Dinner

POTATO PIZZAS

When not laden with fatty sausage, a heavy layer of high-fat cheese and lots of oil, a pizza makes an ideal dinner. This vegetable-topped version is a good source of niacin and potassium, and it also supplies more than 4 grams of dietary fibre per serving.

CALORIES per serving	400
72% Carbohydrate	72 g
11% Protein	11 g
17% Fat	8 g
CALCIUM	56 mg
IRON	4 mg
SODIUM	341 mg

7 g (¼ oz) dried yeast
350 g (12 oz) plain flour
15 g (½ oz) margarine, melted
½ teaspoon salt, approximately
250 g (8 oz) small red potatoes
1 red onion
4 firm ripe plum tomatoes

1 tablespoon cornmeal
1 tablespoon olive oil
1 tablespoon grated Parmesan
1 teaspoon dried oregano
¼ teaspoon ground pepper
4 tablespoons chopped parsley

Place the yeast in a large bowl and add 15 cl (¼ pint) of warm water (40-45°C/105-115°F); stir to combine, then set aside for 3 to 5 minutes. Add 45 g (1½ oz) of flour and stir until smooth, then add the margarine, ½ teaspoon of salt and the remaining flour, and stir until the mixture forms a cohesive dough. Transfer the dough to a lightly floured surface and knead for 5 to 10

Potato Pizzas

minutes, until the dough is smooth and elastic. Place the dough in a medium-sized bowl, cover it with a damp tea towel and set it aside in a warm place to rise for 1 hour, or until doubled in bulk. Meanwhile, wash the potatoes, place them in a small saucepan with cold water to cover and bring to the boil over medium-high heat. Reduce the heat and simmer, uncovered, for 10 to 15 minutes, until the potatoes are just tender when pierced with a sharp knife. Drain the potatoes and set them aside to cool.

When the dough has risen, knock it back and divide it into four. Wrap each piece in plastic film and refrigerate until needed. Peel the onion, then cut the tomatoes, onion and potatoes into 5 mm (¼ inch) thick slices; set aside.

Preheat the oven to 240°C (475°F or Mark 9). Dust the work surface and a rolling pin with cornmeal. Roll each portion of dough into a ball, flatten it into a disc, then roll it out to an 18 cm (7 inch) circle about 3 mm (⅛ inch) thick. Place the circles of dough on a non-stick baking sheet. Top each pizza base with onions, then with potato and tomato slices. Dribble olive oil over the pizzas, then sprinkle each one with some of the Parmesan, oregano and pepper and a pinch of salt. Bake the pizzas for 10 minutes, then reduce the oven temperature to 200°C (400°F or Mark 6) and bake for 5 to 7 minutes more, until the crusts are golden. Sprinkle the pizzas with the parsley, and serve.

Makes 4 servings

SPAGHETTI WITH TURKEY-TOMATO SAUCE

White turkey meat has the lowest fat content of any meat or poultry. Substituting turkey for minced beef or sausage-meat in a pasta sauce and adding lots of vegetables are two easy ways to make a healthier sauce.

CALORIES per serving	425
72% Carbohydrate	77 g
13% Protein	14 g
15% Fat	7 g
CALCIUM	90 mg
IRON	4 mg
SODIUM	268 mg

60 g (2 oz) minced turkey
1 tablespoon plus
   1 teaspoon chopped garlic
1 teaspoon dried oregano
¼ teaspoon pepper
Pinch of salt
2 tablespoons olive oil
250 g (8 oz) onions, chopped

90 g (3 oz) celery, chopped
90 g (3 oz) carrots, chopped
1 bay leaf
850 g (28 oz) canned plum
   tomatoes, with their liquid
1 tablespoon cornflour
550 g (18 oz) spaghetti
1 tablespoon chopped parsley

In a small bowl, stir together the turkey, 1 teaspoon of garlic, ½ teaspoon of oregano, the pepper and salt. Cover loosely and set aside. For the sauce, heat the oil in a medium-sized saucepan over medium heat, add the onions and the remaining garlic, and sauté for 5 minutes, or until the onions are translucent. Add the celery, carrots, bay leaf and remaining oregano. Reserving 12.5 cl (4 fl oz) of their liquid, add the tomatoes and remaining liquid to the pan and bring to the boil over medium-high heat. Cover the pan, reduce the heat to low and simmer the sauce for 10 minutes. Meanwhile, stir together in a cup the cornflour and reserved tomato liquid.

Increase the heat to medium high, bring the sauce to the boil and stir in the cornflour mixture. Add the turkey, breaking it up with a spoon. Reduce the heat to medium low, partially cover the pan and simmer the sauce for 15 minutes more. Meanwhile, bring a large pan of water to the boil and cook the spaghetti for 10 to 12 minutes, or according to the packet directions, until *al dente*. Drain the spaghetti and divide it among six plates. Top each serving with some sauce, sprinkle with the parsley and serve. Makes 6 servings

FETTUCCINE WITH VEGETABLES

Pasta is a good source of riboflavin, which aids in energy metabolism.

CALORIES per serving	495
72% Carbohydrate	90 g
18% Protein	23 g
10% Fat	6 g
CALCIUM	157 mg
IRON	4 mg
SODIUM	340 mg

250 g (8 oz) French beans
250 g (8 oz) yellow courgettes
200 g (7 oz) low-fat cottage cheese
15 cl (¼ pint) skimmed milk
2 tablespoons chopped parsley
15 g (½ oz) margarine
250 g (8 oz) red onions, sliced
2 garlic cloves, chopped

350 g (12 oz) fettuccine
250 g (8 oz) frozen sweetcorn kernels
½ teaspoon dried summer savory or basil
¼ teaspoon white pepper
Pinch of salt
1 tablespoon grated Parmesan

Wash and trim the beans and courgettes. Cut the beans into 5 cm (2 inch) lengths. Cut the courgettes into 5 mm (¼ inch) thick slices; set aside. Process the cottage cheese in a blender until smooth. With the machine running, add the milk, and process for 5 seconds. Stir in the parsley; set aside.

Bring a large pan of water to the boil. Meanwhile, melt the margarine in a medium-sized frying pan over medium heat. Add the onion and garlic, and cook, stirring, for 5 minutes. Cook the fettuccine in the boiling water for 8 to 10 minutes, or according to the packet directions, until *al dente*. Meanwhile, add the beans, courgettes, sweetcorn, savory, pepper and salt to the frying pan, and cook, stirring frequently, for about 10 minutes, or until the vegetables are tender but still crisp.

Drain the pasta and transfer it to a serving bowl. Add the cheese sauce and vegetables, and toss to combine. Sprinkle the pasta and vegetables with the Parmesan, and serve immediately. Makes 4 servings

RATATOUILLE SOUP

Calcium and potassium, both vital to muscle function, are abundantly supplied by the vegetables in this soup.

CALORIES per serving	165
78% Carbohydrate	36 g
15% Protein	7 g
7% Fat	1 g
CALCIUM	212 mg
IRON	5 mg
SODIUM	42 mg

250 g (8 oz) aubergine
175 g (6 oz) courgettes
125 g (4 oz) carrots
125 g (4 oz) onions
2 garlic cloves
850 g (28 oz) canned tomatoes, with their liquid

2 tablespoons chopped parsley
1 teaspoon dried basil
½ teaspoon dried oregano
⅛ teaspoon ground pepper
Pinch of sugar
1 bay leaf

Trim and dice the aubergine, courgettes and carrots. Peel and coarsely chop the onions and garlic; set aside. Place the tomatoes and their liquid in a medium-sized saucepan and bring to the boil over medium-high heat. Add the prepared vegetables, the parsley, basil, oregano, pepper, sugar and bay leaf. Cover the pan, reduce the heat to medium low and simmer for 30 minutes.

Remove the pan from the heat and allow the soup to cool slightly; remove and discard the bay leaf. Transfer 75 cl (24 fl oz) of the solids to a food processor or blender and process for 1 minute, or until coarsely puréed. Return the purée to the pan and stir to combine. Reheat the soup and serve it hot; alternatively, serve it well chilled. Makes 2 servings

Biscotti

Desserts

BISCOTTI

The dried fruit in these biscuits is a good source of magnesium.

450 g (15 oz) plain flour
1 teaspoon baking powder
Pinch of salt
75 g (2½ oz) margarine
125 g (4 oz) sugar
3 eggs

1 tablespoon grated lemon rind
1 tablespoon lemon juice
¾ teaspoon anise extract
150 g (5 oz) currants
125 g (4 oz) dried apricots,
    chopped

CALORIES per biscuit	70
71% Carbohydrate	12 g
8% Protein	1 g
21% Fat	2 g
CALCIUM	12 mg
IRON	1 mg
SODIUM	31 mg

Preheat the oven to 180°C (350°F or Mark 4). In a medium-sized bowl, combine the flour, baking powder and salt; set aside. In another medium-sized bowl, cream the margarine and sugar, using an electric mixer. Beat in the eggs, one at a time, then beat in the lemon rind and juice and the anise extract. Gradually add the dry ingredients, beating constantly for 1 to 2 minutes, until almost incorporated. Add the currants and apricots, and beat for 1 minute more, or until just combined. Divide the dough in two and shape into 6 cm (2½ inch) thick loaves. Place them on a non-stick baking sheet and bake for 30 minutes, or until just beginning to brown. Allow the loaves to cool on a rack for 45 minutes.

Preheat the grill. Place the loaves on a cutting board and, with a serrated knife, cut them diagonally into 1 cm (½ inch) thick slices. Lay them on a baking sheet and grill 12 cm (5 inches) from the heat for 1 minute, or until lightly browned. Turn them carefully and brown for another minute. Cool on a rack, then store in an airtight container. Makes 48 biscotti

CALORIES per biscuit	30
86% Carbohydrate	6 g
7% Protein	1 g
7% Fat	0.2 g
CALCIUM	14 mg
IRON	Trace
SODIUM	18 mg

APPLE-PUMPKIN CHEWIES

These soft biscuits pack well, making them a good choice for a hike or picnic dessert. The pumpkin keeps them moist and is an excellent source of vitamin A, which plays a role in glycogen synthesis.

2 large Granny Smith apples	½ teaspoon pure vanilla extract
250 g (8 oz) canned pumpkin	150 g (5 oz) plain flour
1 egg, lightly beaten	15 g (½ oz) rolled oats
4 tablespoons molasses	1½ teaspoons baking powder
4 tablespoons brown sugar	½ teaspoon ground ginger
1 teaspoon grated lemon rind	Pinch of salt

Preheat the oven to 180°C (350°F or Mark 4). Lightly oil a baking sheet; set aside. Core but do not peel the apples, then grate them into a medium-sized bowl. Add the pumpkin, egg, molasses, sugar, lemon rind and vanilla and stir to combine; set aside. In a large bowl, stir together the flour, oats, baking powder, ginger and salt, and make a well in the centre. Add the apple mixture and stir until just combined. Drop the batter by tablespoons on to the baking sheet and bake for 35 minutes, or until the biscuits are golden. Transfer the biscuits to a rack to cool. Repeat with the remaining batter. If not serving immediately, store the biscuits in an airtight container. When fresh, they have a moist centre; after a few days they will be chewier. Makes 48 biscuits

MOLASSES BISCUITS

White sugar is made of carbohydrate, but has no other nutritional value. Molasses, however, contains trace amounts of the minerals potassium, calcium and iron.

165 g (5½ oz) light molasses	4 tablespoons brown sugar
75 g (2½ oz) margarine, cut into	1 tablespoon skimmed milk
15 g (½ oz) pieces	1 teaspoon ground ginger
300 g (10 oz) plain flour	½ teaspoon baking powder

Heat the molasses in a medium-sized saucepan over medium-low heat. When the molasses reaches boiling point, stir in the margarine. When the margarine has melted, remove the pan from the heat and stir in the flour, sugar, milk, ginger and baking powder. Stir until the mixture forms a thick dough that pulls away from the sides of the pan. Place the dough on a 30 cm (12 inch) square sheet of foil and let it cool for a few minutes, then form it into a 4 cm (1½ inch) thick roll about 25 cm (10 inches) long. Wrap the dough in the foil and refrigerate it for at least 3 hours, until firm.

Preheat the oven to 170°C (325°F or Mark 3). Unwrap the dough and, with a sharp knife, cut it into 5 mm (¼ inch) thick slices. (Dip the knife briefly into warm water between cuts if the dough sticks to it.) Place the biscuits 2.5 cm (1 inch) apart on a non-stick baking sheet and bake for 10 to 15 minutes, until just firm to the touch. Transfer the biscuits to a rack to cool; if not serving immediately, store in an airtight container. Makes 40 biscuits

CALORIES per biscuit	50
68% Carbohydrate	9 g
5% Protein	1 g
27% Fat	2 g
CALCIUM	13 mg
IRON	Trace
SODIUM	24 mg

PEAR CUPCAKES

These low-fat, high-fibre cupcakes are a healthy dessert alternative to a slice of iced cake. Skimmed milk is an excellent dietary source of calcium, which is important in neuromuscular functioning and in the breakdown of glycogen in the muscles as well as in maintaining bone density and overall strength.

1 firm ripe Comice pear
300 g (10 oz) plain flour
60 g (2 oz) cornmeal
2 teaspoons baking powder
5 teaspoons margarine

50 g (2 oz) brown sugar
1 egg, lightly beaten
½ teaspoon orange extract
½ teaspoon grated orange rind
25 cl (8 fl oz) skimmed milk

Preheat the oven to 190°C (375°F or Mark 5). Line 12 deep bun tin cups with paper liners; set aside. Core but do not peel the pear, then grate it into a small bowl. In another small bowl, combine the flour, cornmeal and baking powder; set aside. In a medium-sized bowl, cream together the margarine and sugar, then gradually beat in the egg, orange extract and orange rind. Stir in the pear, then add half the milk and half the dry ingredients, and stir to combine. Add the remaining milk and dry ingredients, and stir until just combined; do not overmix. Divide the batter among the bun tin cups (they will be about three-quarters full) and bake for 30 to 35 minutes, until the cupcakes are golden and a toothpick inserted in a cupcake comes out clean and dry. Transfer the cupcakes to a rack to cool before serving.   Makes 12 cupcakes

CALORIES per cupcake	155
78% Carbohydrate	30 g
10% Protein	4 g
12% Fat	2 g
CALCIUM	74 mg
IRON	1 mg
SODIUM	105 mg

APPLE FREEZE

Most fruit-based frozen desserts are higher in carbohydrates than ice cream, but some contain double cream and are high in fat. This smooth but nearly fat-free dessert is made with low-fat yogurt, and including the apple peels makes it high in pectin, an especially beneficial form of dietary fibre.

1.25 kg (2½ lb) apples,
    preferably a combination of
    Granny Smith and Red Delicious
100 g (3½ oz) caster sugar
2 tablespoons lemon juice

12.5 cl (4 fl oz) plain low-fat
    yogurt
1 egg white
¼ teaspoon ground cinnamon

Core but do not peel the apples, and cut them into chunks. Process them in a food processor or blender for 1 to 2 minutes, until puréed. Add the sugar and lemon juice, and process for another minute, or until well blended. Add the remaining ingredients, and process for 1 minute more. Transfer the mixture to the container of an ice-cream maker and freeze it for 20 minutes, or according to the manufacturer's instructions, until firm.

If not serving the apple freeze immediately, cover the container tightly and place it in the freezer. If necessary, let it soften at room temperature for 5 minutes, or until soft enough to scoop, before serving. Divide the apple freeze among eight dessert bowls, and serve.   Makes 8 servings

CALORIES per serving	135
92% Carbohydrate	34 g
4% Protein	1.5 g
4% Fat	0.6 g
CALCIUM	37 mg
IRON	3 mg
SODIUM	17 mg

Snacks

CORN THINS

Unlike many packaged snacks, these savoury biscuits are low in sodium.

CALORIES per biscuit	10
76% Carbohydrate	2 g
9% Protein	0.2 g
15% Fat	0.2 g
CALCIUM	2 mg
IRON	Trace
SODIUM	15 mg

125 g (4 oz) cornmeal
75 g (2½ oz) plain flour
1 tablespoon sugar
½ teaspoon salt
¼ teaspoon bicarbonate of soda

¼ teaspoon ground pepper, or
  more to taste
12.5 cl (4 fl oz) plain low-fat
  yogurt
15 g (½ oz) margarine, melted

Preheat the oven to 180°C (350°F or Mark 4). In a medium-sized bowl, combine the cornmeal, flour, sugar, salt, bicarbonate of soda and pepper. Add the yogurt and margarine and stir until combined. Divide the dough into two portions. Lightly oil a baking sheet; lightly dust a rolling pin with cornmeal. Place one portion of dough on the baking sheet and roll it out to a 5 mm (¼ inch) thickness. Place a sheet of plastic film over the dough and roll it out to a 25 cm (10 inch) square. Remove the plastic film. Using a ruler and a sharp knife, cut the dough into 5 cm (2 inch) squares, then into triangles; do not separate them. Bake for 20 minutes, or until crisp and golden. Check after 8 minutes; if the biscuits are browning unevenly, turn the baking sheet. With a metal spatula, transfer the biscuits to a rack to cool (they will separate as you remove them from the sheet). Wash and re-oil the baking sheet, then make a second batch of corn thins in the same way.   Makes 100 biscuits

Corn Thins

ALMOST-CHOCOLATE BUNS

The rich flavour of dark rye bread, combined with vanilla, gives these buns a chocolate-like taste. They freeze well and are good to have on hand for a quick carbohydrate boost before or after exercise. A bought chocolate cupcake would have about twice the fat and one quarter the calcium.

CALORIES per bun	**140**
74% Carbohydrate	27 g
12% Protein	4 g
14% Fat	2 g
CALCIUM	89 mg
IRON	1 mg
SODIUM	243 mg

**Crumbs from 6 slices of fresh
   dark rye bread**
150 g (5 oz) plain flour
2 teaspoons baking powder
¼ teaspoon salt

2 eggs
75 g (2½ oz) brown sugar
15 g (½ oz) margarine, melted
1 teaspoon pure vanilla extract
25 cl (8 fl oz) skimmed milk

Preheat the oven to 190°C (375°F or Mark 5). Line 12 deep bun tin cups with paper liners; set aside. In a medium-sized bowl, combine the breadcrumbs, flour, baking powder and salt; set aside. Beat the eggs in another medium-sized bowl, then beat in the sugar, margarine and vanilla. Add half of the milk, then half of the dry ingredients, and stir until combined. Add the remaining milk and dry ingredients and stir until just combined; do not overmix. Divide the batter among the bun tin cups (they will be about three-quarters full) and bake for 25 minutes, or until the buns are brown and a toothpick inserted in a bun comes out clean and dry. Transfer the buns to a rack to cool before serving.

Makes 12 buns

DOSAS

In India, the griddle breads called dosas are served plain or stuffed with a filling such as spiced potatoes. The Vegetable Purée on page 131 would make a good topping for these multi-grain breads. You could also use cottage cheese with a pinch of curry powder mixed in. For a sweet snack, you might spread the dosas with Chunky Fruit Butter (page 131) or crushed berries.

CALORIES per dosa	**105**
84% Carbohydrate	22 g
12% Protein	3 g
4% Fat	1 g
CALCIUM	30 mg
IRON	1 mg
SODIUM	103 mg

165 g (5½ oz) cornmeal
45 g (1½ oz) wholemeal flour
45 g (1½ oz) plain flour
½ teaspoon salt

**100 g (3½ oz) cooked brown rice
   (45 g/1½ oz raw)**
25 cl (8 fl oz) skimmed milk

In a medium-sized bowl, combine the cornmeal, wholemeal flour, plain flour and salt. Add the rice, milk and 17.5 cl (6 fl oz) of water, and stir until the mixture forms a batter. Cover the bowl with plastic film and set aside at room temperature for 1 hour.

Lightly oil a large frying pan and heat it over medium-high heat. Pour in scant 4-tablespoon portions of batter and cook them for about 2½ minutes, or until tiny holes form on the surface and the batter appears slightly dry. Turn the dosas and cook for another 2 minutes, or until the second side is dry. Repeat with the remaining batter. Serve the dosas hot or warm; they may also be eaten cold but they will not be as tender.

Makes 12 dosas

ACKNOWLEDGEMENTS

The editors wish to thank Norma MacMillan.

Nutritional analyses provided by Hill Nutrition Associates, New York State.

Index prepared by Ian Tucker.

PHOTOGRAPHY CREDITS

Indoor exercise photography and photograph on page 6: Andrew Eccles; outdoor photography: © David Madison 1988; photographs on pages 90, 91, 104, 105: © David Epperson/WILDPIC.

ILLUSTRATION CREDITS

Pages 8, 9, 10, illustrations: David Flaherty; page 14, chart, illustration: Phil Scheuer; pages 19, 20, 21, 23, charts: Brian Sisco; pages 78, 90, 91, illustrations: Phil Scheuer; pages 108, 109, 110, 113, charts: Brian Sisco.

Typeset by A.J. Latham Limited,
Dunstable, Bedfordshire, England
Printed by GEA, Milan and bound by GEP,
Cremona, Italy

INDEX